SFLEP Biography Titles 英汉对照/外教社人物传记丛书（第二辑）

NELSON MANDELA
纳尔逊·曼德拉

Reggie Finlayson

丘月关 李 欣 译注

U0783602

上海外语教育出版社
外教社 SHANGHAI FOREIGN LANGUAGE EDUCATION PRESS

Lerner Publications Company

图书在版编目（CIP）数据

纳尔逊·曼德拉/（美）芬利森（Finlayson, R.）著；丘月
关、李欣译注. —上海：上海外语教育出版社，2008（**2011**重印）
（外教社人物传记丛书. 第2辑）
ISBN 978–7–5446–0903–6

Ⅰ. 纳⋯　Ⅱ.①芬⋯②丘⋯③李⋯　Ⅲ.曼德拉，N.—传记
Ⅳ. K834.787=5

中国版本图书馆 CIP 数据核字（2008）第 104028 号

图字：09–2007–688 号

图片来源/东方 IC

出版发行： 上海外语教育出版社
（上海外国语大学内）　邮编：200083
电　　话：021–65425300（总机）
电子邮箱：bookinfo@sflep.com.cn
网　　址：http://www.sflep.com.cn　　http://www.sflep.com
责任编辑：徐　喆

印　　刷：常熟市华顺印刷有限公司
开　　本：850×1168　1/32　印张5　字数153千字
版　　次：2008 年 10 月第 1 版　2011 年 12 月第 2 次印刷
印　　数：3 100 册

书　　号：ISBN 978-7-5446-0903-6 / K · 0016
定　　价：20.00 元

本版图书如有印装质量问题，可向本社调换

Biography 外教社人物传记丛书

出版前言

　　曾经有人做了一项调查，拥有最多读者的书籍是传记。阅读一本优秀的人物传记，往往可以使人振作精神，奋发图强，尤其对于青少年，阅读传记更可以使他们建立起正确的人生坐标，从而开拓美好的未来。

　　上海外语教育出版社从美国乐勒出版集团引进的"外教社人物传记丛书"就是这样一套奉献给青少年朋友的优秀传记丛书。本丛书第一辑13册自2006年初问世以来，得到了广大青年读者的认可和好评。为满足他们了解优秀人物、获取精神财富的需求，我社今年又隆重推出该丛书第二辑13册，包括诺贝尔和平奖获得者德兰修女、曼德拉，政坛风云人物拿破仑、丘吉尔，文学巨匠马克·吐温和简·奥斯丁，天才科学家霍金，影视娱乐界巨星乔治·卢卡斯、克里斯托弗·里夫和奥普拉·温弗瑞，环法自行车赛冠军兰斯·阿姆斯特朗，以及世界历史上著名的两位女王——伊丽莎白一世和克娄巴特拉。阅读这些著名人物的传奇人生，可以帮助青少年朋友们了解西方不同时代的社会历史背景，更能激励他们树立远大理想，以积极的态度直面人生的风雨。

　　这套传记丛书均由专门从事青少年文学创作的美国资深作家撰写，语言生动活泼，故事性强，引人入胜。外教社特邀一批在翻译方面颇有建树的年轻学者对丛书进行翻译和注释，希望英汉对照加注释这一形式能更好地帮助读者学习英语，享受阅读。

　　这套丛书特别适合高中生和大学一二年级的学生阅读。我们相信它必将成为青少年朋友们学习英语、探求人生真谛的好伙伴！

上海外语教育出版社

2008 年 1 月

NELSON MANDELA

Contents

Biography 外 教 社

纳尔逊·曼德拉

目 录

人物传记丛书

CHAPTER ONE

A TURNING POINT IN HISTORY

历史的转折点

The morning of May 10, 1994, was bright and clear. Leaders from around the world had gathered in Pretoria, South Africa, for the largest international gathering ever held on the African continent. The air crackled[1] with excitement as visitors from Europe, Asia, Africa, and America took their places. Blacks and whites sat side by side in the glistening[2] sandstone amphitheater[3]. Few could have imagined such a scene a decade earlier, when South Africa was locked in a titanic[4] and violent struggle between the races. But that time was a memory that many hoped would quickly fade. The world's leaders were in Pretoria to mark the change.

The assembled leaders were indeed impressive—but not nearly as impressive as the historic event they had come to honor. They were witnessing nothing short of the birth of a new nation.

Like a lion, Nelson Rolihlahla Mandela, newly elected president of South Africa, strode across the stage to the podium[5], and all eyes followed him in silence. There was a youthful spring in his step—despite his seventy-six years, despite the nearly three decades he had spent in South African prisons. He greeted the audience with open arms. It was easy to see how his name had become a rallying call, his face a symbol of survival,

his spirit the very essense of freedom. As he acknowledged kings and queens, presidents and prime ministers, they leaned forward in their seats so as not to miss a word.

"Today, all of us do, by our presence here, and by our celebration in other parts of our country and the world, confer[6] glory and hope to newborn liberty," Mandela intoned[7] with a voice full of a strange power. It

[1] crackled 充满
生气（或不安、
紧张等）

[2] glistening （因
有水珠、光滑等
而）发亮的

[3] amphitheater
圆形露天体育
场（或剧场）

[4] titanic 范围、
力量或影响巨
大的

[5] podium 讲台

[6] confer 授予；
赋予

[7] intoned 吟咏，
吟诵

纳尔逊·曼德拉

1994年5月10日的早晨，天空明净。世界各国首脑在南非比勒陀利亚济济一堂，参加非洲大陆上有史以来最高级别的国际盛会。处处充满着勃勃生气，来自欧洲、亚洲、非洲以及美洲的来宾各就各位。用沙岩建造的圆形露天体育场内熠熠生辉，黑人与白人并肩而坐。此情此景，在10年前几乎没人能想像，那时的南非深陷于严重而激烈的种族冲突中。但那是一段许多人都希望忘却的记忆。世界各国的领导人聚集在比勒陀利亚，正是为了见证历史的变化。

如此多的领袖聚首一处，这本身已让人印象深刻——但仍无法与他们即将目睹的历史事件相提并论。他们将要见证的无异于一个全新国家的诞生。

就像一头雄狮，纳尔逊·罗利赫拉赫拉·曼德拉——新当选的南非总统——大踏步穿过舞台，走向讲台，所有人都静静地注视着他。他的步伐充满青春的活力——即便他已是76岁高龄，即便他生命中将近30个年头在南非的监狱中度过。他伸出双臂迎接每一位听众。显而易见，他的名字如此具有号召力，他的面孔就是生命力的象征，他的精神成了自由的本质。当他向在场的国王、女王、总统、首相致意时，他们一个个全都在座位上把身子往前倾，唯恐漏掉他所说出的任何一个词。

"今天，我们所有的人，或聚首于此，或在这个国家的其他地方以及世界各地举行庆祝活动，借此将荣耀与希望赋予刚诞生的自由，"曼德拉的语调充满异乎寻常的力量。最迟钝的

was clear, even to the most insensitive, that this was not just another inauguration[1] speech. In his words could be heard the echo of generations of South Africans, alive and dead, who had struggled to be free. His voice seemed infused[2] with the voices of those who had been massacred[3] in Sharpeville and Soweto—of Steven Biko and thousands of others who had been detained, beaten, and even killed—the voices of all the restless souls who had died to change the nation.

But Mandela's words were also charged with the compassion of a man who had known too much violence and hatred. "We have triumphed in the effort to implant hope in the breasts of the millions of our people," he said. "We enter into a covenant[4] that we shall build the society in which all South Africans, both black and white, will be able to walk tall, without any fear in their hearts, assured of their unalienable[5] right to human dignity—a rainbow nation at peace with itself and the world."

The audience nodded, sighed, and clapped. Mandela's own example offered hope to not only South Africans but also to the world at large. He had stood up to forces of oppression and spent more than a quarter of a century in prison for his trouble. Yet he had come out unbowed and prepared to continue the struggle. At a point in life when most men retire, Nelson Mandela took the helm[6] of a new nation. He had traveled a long way—and crossed many famous rivers.

NELSON MANDELA

[1] inauguration
就职典礼

[2] infused 充满

[3] massacred 大
屠杀

[4] covenant 公
约，盟约；契约

[5] unalienable
不可剥夺的

[6] helm （政府、
组织等的）领导
地位

人也能立即感受到，这绝不是例行公事的就职演讲。从他的话语中可以感受到几代南非人民发自心灵深处的呐喊，他们有的依然健在，有的已经死去，但他们都曾经为自由而奋斗。他的声音中似乎融入了许许多多人的声音：融入了那些在沙佩维尔和索韦托遭大屠杀者的声音；融入了斯蒂文·比科以及千千万万遭囚禁、遭殴打，甚至遭谋杀者的声音；融入了那些为了改变这个国家而永远战斗、至死不渝的先驱们的声音。

除此之外，曼德拉的话语同样饱含着怜悯，这是一个经历了太多暴力与仇恨的人内心的怜悯。"我们已经成功地使这个国家几百万人民的心中充满了希望，"他说。"我们订立了公约，将建立起一个所有南非人的社会，无论是黑人还是白人，都能够挺直腰板，心中不再存有畏惧，他们作为人的不可剥夺的尊严将得到保障。对它自身以及整个世界来说，这将是一个充满和平的理想之国。"

所有的听众点头，发出感叹，掌声不断。曼德拉自身的榜样，不仅为南非，而且为整个世界都带来了希望。面对压迫，他勇敢地站出来，并因此在囚牢中度过了超过四分之一个世纪。然而，他不屈地回来了，并准备继续抗争。在一个绝大多数人早已退休的年龄，纳尔逊·曼德拉获得了一个全新国家的至高领导权。他的人生旅途如此漫长——并趟过了许多著名的"湍流"。

纳尔逊·曼德拉

CHAPTER TWO
BIRTH OF A LEADER
领袖的诞生

Rolihlahla Mandela was born on July 18, 1918, in the small village of Mvezo in South Africa. This rural community sits in an area full of rolling hills, fertile valleys, and generous streams. It is about 800 miles east of Cape Town, 550 miles south of Johannesburg, and next to the blue waters of the Indian Ocean. This land, called the Transkei region, is the traditional homeland of the Xhosa, one of the largest ethnic groups in South Africa.

Rolihlahla was born into the Thembu clan[1] within the Xhosa nation. From the beginning, he was steeped[2] in the culture of this group. At birth, he was not called Nelson, the name by which he later became known. Instead, he bore the traditional Xhosa name Rolihlahla. According to custom, Xhosa people were given names that described them in some way or suggested what they might become. Rolihlahla meant "pulling the branch of a tree." Gadla Henry Mphakanyiswa, Rolihlahla's father, gave this name to his son.

Rolihlahla was born into a royal Xhosa family. Gadla Henry Mphakanyiswa was a minor chief in the village of Mvezo. Like a mayor, he kept business moving in the village and settled disputes. When necessary, he assumed the role of judge and decided cases according to tribal law. Finally, he served as something of a prime minister, or chief adviser, to the highest tribal authority, the Thembu king.

Rolihlahla loved his father and was very proud of his experience, his wisdom, and the way people in the community looked up to him. The man provided the first lessons in leadership for his son.

罗利赫拉赫拉·曼德拉1918年7月18日生于南非姆维座的一个小村庄。村庄四周满是连绵的小山、肥沃的山谷，还有川流不息的小河。村庄位于开普敦以东约800英里，约翰内斯堡以南550英里，濒临蓝色的印度洋。这里被称为特兰斯凯地区，是南非最主要的民族之一——科萨人——的聚居地。

罗利赫拉赫拉出生于坦布氏族，该氏族是科萨部落的一个分支。从出生开始，他就受到氏族文化的熏陶。他的原名并非人们熟知的纳尔逊，而是一个传统的科萨名字，罗利赫拉赫拉。根据传统，科萨人的名字都有某种含义，可能是对他们自己某种特点的描述，或者是对他们将来的某种期望。罗利赫拉赫拉的意思是"拉扯树枝"。这个名字是罗利赫拉赫拉·曼德拉的父亲——盖拉·亨利·穆帕卡尼斯瓦——起的。

罗利赫拉赫拉出生在一个科萨部落的王室家庭。父亲盖拉·亨利·穆帕卡尼斯瓦是姆维座村的一个小头领。他负责保障村里的商业活动和处理纠纷，职权类似于市长。如果有必要，他还要担当法官，根据部落法律对纠纷进行裁决。最后，他还要为部落最高权威——坦布首领——充当类似首相或是首席顾问的角色。

罗利赫拉赫拉很爱父亲，为父亲的经历、智慧以及当地居民对他的仰慕感到骄傲。父亲给罗利赫拉赫拉上了关于领导能力的第一课。

[1] clan 氏族，部族；家族

[2] steeped 浸泡，浸透；沾染

纳尔逊·曼德拉

"In later years, I discovered that my father was not only an adviser to kings but a king-maker," Nelson Rolihlahla Mandela later wrote in his autobiography[1], *Long Walk to Freedom*. He explained that in the 1920s, the Xhosa king Jongilizwe had died unexpectedly. The heir apparent had been too young to assume the throne, and a dispute had broken out over which other heir should claim the role in the interim[2]. Rolihlahla's father took a controversial stance[3] to support a man who was fairly low in the pecking order[4] but who was the best educated—a man named Jongintaba.

Mphakanyiswa's opinion carried the day[5], and Jongintaba was installed[6] as acting king, or regent[7]. The elders soon applauded the decision—and the wisdom and good fortune Jongintaba would bring to the Xhosa people. As it turned out, the choice would also make a difference for the Mandela family. But that would be years in coming.

A Legacy of Struggle

During Rolihlahla's youth, his society was changing rapidly. The old tribal ways were yielding to new ideas about religion, housing, clothing, and marriage. Many neighbors threw out the old ideas, but Rolihlahla's father held fast to the traditional way of life.

According to custom, Mphakanyiswa had four wives. Rolihlahla's

mother, Nosekeni Fanny, was the third. Rolihlahla was the oldest of his mother's children but the youngest male among all his father's children. Between the four wives, Mphakanyiswa produced thirteen children: four boys and nine girls.

The entire family did not live together under one roof. Each wife had her own kraal[8], a rural homestead that included fields for

"多年之后，我发觉，其实父亲不仅仅担当了首领智囊的角色，他甚至还是首领制造者，"纳尔逊·罗利赫拉赫拉·曼德拉后来在他的自传《漫漫自由路》中如此写道。他就此解释说，20世纪20年代时，科萨氏族首领容吉里兹瓦意外死亡，而首领的第一继承人还很年幼，无法继承王位。于是过渡期里由谁来掌权的问题引起了纷争。罗利赫拉赫拉的父亲的态度引起了争议，他支持一个叫容欣塔巴的人。容欣塔巴当时在部落中地位较低，但却是受教育的程度最高的一个。

穆帕卡尼斯瓦的意见最终胜出，于是容欣塔巴成为了代理首领，也就是摄政王。氏族长老们很快就为这一决定喝彩了——为容欣塔巴给科萨人带来的智慧与好运喝彩。结果，这一决定还对曼德拉家庭产生了影响，但那是多年以后的事了。

抗争的传承

青少年时代，罗利赫拉赫拉所处的社会急剧变化着，古老的部落传统不断被新思想蚕食，包括宗教、住所、衣着乃至婚姻的方方面面都在改变。许多邻居抛弃旧思想，然而罗利赫拉赫拉的父亲始终固守着传统的生活方式。

根据风俗，穆帕卡尼斯瓦有4位妻子。罗利赫拉赫拉的生母，诺塞凯尼·范妮，排第三位。罗利赫拉赫拉是他母亲的长子，而在他父亲的所有孩子中，他是最小的一个男孩。4位妻子一共为穆帕卡尼斯瓦生了13个子女：4个男孩，9个女孩。

整个大家庭并非住在同一屋檐下，每一位妻子都有她自己的村庄——农村家宅，包括几块耕地、

[1] autobiography
自传

[2] interim 过渡
时期

[3] stance 态度

[4] pecking order
（任何团体中的）长幼尊卑制度，权势等级

[5] carried the day
获胜，占优势

[6] installed 任命

[7] regent 摄政者

[8] kraal （南非土人用栅栏围起来的）栅栏村庄

farming, a pen[1] for animals, and one or more thatched[2] huts for living space. The kraals of the four wives were similar but were separated by several miles. Rolihlahla's father divided his time equally between them.

Mphakanyiswa was a proud man. He was wealthy by Xhosa standards and respected in his community. He drew pay as a local chief and enjoyed the status that went along with it. But even a wealthy and respected Xhosa man did not have all that much status in South African society.

The population of South Africa was multiracial. Nearly eighty percent of the people were black and belonged to groups such as the Xhosa, Zulu, Ndebele, San, Venda, Swazi, and Pondo. There were also East Indians, whites, and people of mixed race. Most of the country's whites were Afrikaners[3], also called Boers, descendants[4] of Dutch settlers who traced their history in South Africa back to 1652.

For centuries, the great European nations had competed for control over various parts of Africa. In South Africa, the Dutch eventually lost out[5] to the British. It was the British who continued to control South Africa during Rolihlahla's childhood.

The British recognized the tribal governments of the Xhosa, Zulu, and other African groups—but only in part. Local chiefs reported not only to their tribal kings but also to white magistrates[6] appointed by the

British. These magistrates had more power and status than the tribal authorities, and they had the final say in decision making.

Soon after Rolihlahla was born, his father made the mistake of acting as if he were equal in status to a white magistrate. The offended magistrate charged Mphakanyiswa with not following orders and removed him from office. There was no investigation or

[1] pen 畜栏

[2] thatched 茅草盖的；茅草屋顶的

[3] Afrikaners 南非白人，布尔人（指南非的荷兰人等欧洲移民的后裔）

[4] descendants 后裔；后代

[5] lost out （竞赛）失败

[6] magistrates 地方行政官

纳尔逊·曼德拉

一块圈养牲畜的围栏地、一间或几间供起居用的茅草屋。各个家宅的结构相差不多，但彼此相距几英里远，罗利赫拉赫拉的父亲在每一处家宅居住的时间大致相当。

穆帕卡尼斯瓦是个高傲的人。以科萨的标准，他很富有，也颇受当地人的尊重。他的薪俸和地方长官相当，并享有相应的氏族地位。不过，即使是一个富有并受当地人尊敬的科萨人，在整个南非社会中，其地位也要打折扣。

南非是多民族国家，近8成是黑人，分属于不同民族，如科萨、祖鲁、恩德贝勒、桑、文达、斯威士，以及庞多。另外还有东印度人、白人以及混血人种。南非的大多数白人属于南非白人，也叫布尔人，是荷兰殖民者的后裔，荷兰人于1652年踏上了南非的土地。

几世纪以来，欧洲列强在非洲大地上群雄逐鹿，企图各霸一方。在南非，荷兰人最终被英国人击败。在罗利赫拉赫拉的童年时代，一直是英国人统治着南非。

英国人承认科萨、祖鲁以及其他南非部落的地方政府——但只是部分承认。地方氏族头领不仅要对部落首领负责，也要对英国人指派的白人地方总督负责。这些地方总督比部落政府拥有更大的权力，对地方事务拥有最高裁决权。

罗利赫拉赫拉出生不久，父亲由于自以为可以和一位白人总督平起平坐而犯下错误。受到冒犯的总督以违抗命令为由将他免职。没有任何的调查过程，也没

second chance—as there would have been for a white official. With the stroke of a pen, the magistrate stripped[1] Rolihlahla's father of his position and livelihood.

The magistrate did not, however, take Mphakanyiswa's dignity. Nor did he strip him of pride and respect. Like all modern Xhosa, Rolihlahla's father had learned to cope with hard times. This ability came, at least in part, from a tragic event that had occurred several generations earlier. The event was called the Mfecane.

The Mfecane

In 1857 the Xhosa were a dominant force in eastern South Africa. They had successfully fended off attacks by the British for decades. But the Mfecane, or "great Xhosa cattle killing," would shatter the independence of the Xhosa nation.

The Mfecane began with a young woman named Nongqawuse. She was in her late teens or early twenties at the time and was training to become a shaman[2], or healer. As a shaman, Nongqawuse was skilled at seeing the spiritual causes of diseases and personal troubles.

One day when Nongqawuse was in the forest with her sisters, she heard a voice beckoning her. As she stepped into the bush, she saw three strange figures.

"Who are you?" Nongqawuse shouted.

"We are your ancestors," said the voice. It continued:

Listen carefully. We have come from the land of the dead with a message. The dead ones have taken pity on[3] the Xhosa people and, for the Xhosa people, deliverance[4] is near. On the fourteenth day of next month great miracles shall happen in this land. On

[1] stripped 剥夺

有第二次机会——若换作一位白人长官，就会有调查或第二次机会。仅一纸公文，总督就剥夺了穆帕卡尼斯瓦的职位和生计。

然而，总督没法带走穆帕卡尼斯瓦的尊贵，也没能剥夺他的自豪感与尊严。就像所有的现代科萨人一样，罗利赫拉赫拉的父亲早已学会应付艰难的境况。这种能力，至少部分来自于数代之前的一次悲剧事件。这一事件被称为姆菲卡尼事件。

姆菲卡尼事件

1857 年，科萨部落在南非东部地区占有主导地位。他们抵挡住了英国人长达几十年的进攻。但是姆菲卡尼事件，也被称为"科萨牲畜大屠杀"，却打破了科萨部落的独立。

[2] shaman 萨满教巫师

姆菲卡尼事件要从一个叫农贾乌斯的年轻女子说起，她那时十八九岁或刚刚二十出头，正被训练成为萨满巫师，也叫诊疗者。作为一个萨满巫师，她善于寻找疾病以及个人烦恼的精神诱因。

一天，农贾乌斯和她的姐妹们在一片树林中，她听到有一个声音在召唤她，当她走进一片灌木时，看见三个奇异的人影。

"你们是谁？"农贾乌斯喊道。

"我们是你的祖先，"那个声音说。接着那个声音继续说：

[3] taken pity on 同情

[4] deliverance 解救；释放

仔细听好了。我们是从死亡之地来的，捎来了口信。死去的人们同情科萨部落，科萨人民的救赎为期不远了。下个月的第14天，神

•19•

that day, the sun will rise in the east and the graves of the old chiefs will open and those chiefs will rise in the purity of youth. They shall rule the Xhosa more wisely than they did before and the ground will open like a womb and deliver thousands of cattle. There will be no more rich and poor Xhosa, for everybody will have enough. A great wind will sweep from the north and drive all the white people into the sea and the white race will plague[1] *the Xhosa race no longer.*

But before this can happen, the Xhosa must purify themselves and the whole land. They must show their faith by burning the corn in the fields, killing all the cows and goats, oxen and sheep in their kraals. They must cease eating three times a day and eat only one light meal until the Day of Miracles.

Nongqawuse was speechless when her clansmen arrived just in time to see the three figures depart. One of the clansmen asked the Xhosa king to consider the message from the ancestors. Despite suspicions, the clansman persuaded the king that the instructions by the three ghosts should be followed. The slaughter[2] of animals began almost immediately.

To say the least, there were some who resisted the slaughter, but most who did not were forced to destroy their livestock and crops. There was a madness in the air as the Xhosa people killed their animals.

The real story behind the Mfecane may never be known. Some his-

torians believe that the young woman had been tricked by white settlers or officers of the British government posing as ghosts. What is clear is that after the Mfecane, many Xhosa died of starvation and disease—but that wasn't the worst part.

In the face of the human tragedy, British governor George Grey took advantage of the situation. With the Xhosa weakened by

迹即将降临在这片土地上。在那一天，太阳会从东方升起，已故首领们的墓穴将会洞开，他们将以纯洁的青年之躯复活。他们会以比以前更加智慧的方式统治科萨部落，而且大地会像子宫一样开启，带来数以千计的牲畜。科萨部落从此不会再有富贵和贫穷的差别，因为每个人都将丰衣足食。一阵大风将从北方吹来，将所有白人吹进大海，白人将再也不能折磨科萨部落。

但是，在神迹出现前，科萨部落必须先行净化其自身以及这片土地。他们必须表现出自己的虔诚，把田里的谷物烧掉，杀死村庄里的所有母牛和山羊、阉牛和绵羊。他们必须停止一日三餐，只吃一顿简餐，直到神迹日。

农贾乌斯的族人赶到时，正好看到那3个人影离开，农贾乌斯早已目瞪口呆。一个族人请求科萨首领尊重祖先们的旨意。尽管有怀疑，这个族人说服首领按照那3个鬼魂的话去做。屠杀牲畜的行动几乎立即就开始了。

至少可以说，一部分人拒绝了屠杀牲畜的行动，但大多数人没有拒绝，他们被迫毁灭了自己的牲畜和庄稼。在科萨人对自己的牲畜进行屠杀的过程中，整个部落都笼罩在疯狂的氛围中。

姆菲卡尼事件的幕后真相已无法考证。有些历史学家相信，欺骗年轻女子的鬼魂是白人殖民者或英国政府的官员所装扮的。姆菲卡尼事件造成的后果显而易见，许多科萨人死于饥饿和疾病——但这还不是最糟的。

面对这样的人间悲剧,英国总督乔治·格雷乘虚而入。当科萨部落因饥饿而虚弱时,

[1] plague　折磨

[2] slaughter　屠宰

纳尔逊·曼德拉

hunger, Grey seized their land for whites and drove tens of thousands of Xhosa to work on white-owned farms. The Xhosa had always successfully resisted the British in the past. But the Mfecane broke the back of[1] Xhosa control. The effects could still be felt during Rolihlahla Mandela's youth.

Village Life

Like the Xhosa as a whole, Rolihlahla's father was unable to defy British authorities. Mphakanyiswa was no longer a chief, and with the change in family income, Rolihlahla's mother opted[2] to move her household a few miles away to a smaller village called Qunu. It was nearer to her family and gave her a greater sense of security. In the new village, occupied by just a few hundred people, Rolihlahla's mother had three huts: one for cooking, one for sleeping, and one for storage.

The huts were round structures with mud walls and angled grass roofs supported by wooden poles. The doorways were generally so low that people had to stoop to enter. The huts were set some distance from fields of corn, sorghum[3], beans, and pumpkins. Rolihlahla's family ate what they grew, since imported products were expensive.

Rolihlahla's family did not own their own land, however. The Native Land Act of 1913 had restricted black ownership of land in South Africa. Instead, the government owned the land on which Rolihlahla

lived. In decades to come, the Native Land Act and similar codes would be used to force blacks off their own tribal lands and to strip them of even the most basic rights.

Rolihlahla's childhood, although no longer privileged[4], was a happy one. He was a herd[5] boy who tended sheep and cattle. Like all Xhosa, he learned to love cattle. He felt an almost mystical connection with the

格雷劫掠了科萨人的土地，将其分给白人，还强迫数以万计的科萨人为白人的农场干活。科萨部落以前总是成功击退英国人的进攻，但是姆菲卡尼事件彻底摧垮了科萨部落的统治。事件的影响在罗利赫拉赫拉·曼德拉的青少年时期仍然能够被感受到。

[1] broke the back of 伤及……的要害，摧垮

乡村生活

就像整个科萨部落一样，罗利赫拉赫拉的父亲对英国统治者无能为力。穆帕卡尼斯瓦已经不是首领了，随着家庭经济状况的改变，罗利赫拉赫拉的母亲不得不决定将自己的住所迁至几英里外的一个叫库奴的小村庄。那里离她的娘家比较近，她感觉搬到那里会安全一些。这个陌生的村庄只有几百人，罗利赫拉赫拉的母亲在这里有3间茅屋：一间作厨房，一间用来睡觉，还有一间是储藏室。

[2] opted 选择；作出抉择

这些茅草房是圆形的，墙由泥土砌成，再用木头柱子撑起成角度的茅草屋顶。门非常矮，人必须弯腰才能进出。茅屋离耕地有一段距离，田里种着玉米、高粱、豆子，还有南瓜。罗利赫拉赫拉家吃的都是自己种的食物，因为进口的商品很昂贵。

[3] sorghum 高粱

但是，罗利赫拉赫拉家没有自己的土地。1913年颁布的《黑人土地法》限制黑人在南非拥有土地。罗利赫拉赫拉生活的这片土地归政府所有。自此以后的几十年里，《黑人土地法》以及其他一些类似的法典迫使黑人离开他们世代居住的土地，甚至剥夺了他们最基本的权利。

尽管已经没有任何特权可言，罗利赫拉赫拉的童年时代仍是快乐的。他是个牧童，照看牛羊。就像所有科萨人一样，他学会热爱牛。他觉得自己与这种动物间有某种几乎神秘的联系，

[4] privileged 有特权的
[5] herd 牧群

纳尔逊·曼德拉

animals that was common among his people. To the Xhosa, cattle represented food, wealth, a source of happiness, and a blessing from God.

Nature was Rolihlahla's main teacher, and he absorbed its many lessons. He learned to gather wild honey, to identify edible[1] wild plants, to catch fish with twine[2] and a piece of wire, and to hunt birds with a slingshot[3]. In a time-honored fashion, older herd boys taught Rolihlahla the Xhosa version of a martial art—stick fighting.

Rural life did much to strengthen Rolihlahla's body and sharpen his senses. But it was the traditional Thembu and other Xhosa tales that sparked[4] his imagination and showed him the difference between right and wrong. Rolihlahla listened as the older herd boys told fantastic myths and sat in awe when professional storytellers weaved tales of heroism, sacrifice, and passion. Rolihlahla's favorite stories chronicled[5] the ancient times of the first people in the land.

Qunu was a tightly knit community where people related to one another more as family than as neighbors. Though whites seldom entered this world, the local government representative was white and so was the owner of the nearest store. Occasionally, white travelers and white policemen passed through the small village, but they were rare visitors.

Learning New Lessons

Most of the villagers in Qunu were Xhosa, but there were also some Mfengu, an ethnic group that had migrated into Xhosa territory in the early nineteenth century. Nearly a hundred years later, the Mfengu still lived as a people apart in the land of the Xhosa. Their hosts often looked down on them. Without their own tribal lands, they were at first forced to do the jobs no others would.

这种感觉在他的族人中很常见。对于科萨人来说，牛代表着食物、财富、快乐的源泉，同时也是上帝的赐福。

大自然是罗利赫拉赫拉重要的老师，他从自然中获益匪浅。他学会了采集野蜂蜜，识别能吃的野生植物，用细绳和铁丝捕鱼，用弹弓抓鸟。按照历史悠久的习俗，年长的牧童交给罗利赫拉赫拉一种科萨人的武术——棒术。

乡村生活锻炼了罗利赫拉赫拉的体魄，磨砺了他的意志。然而，是坦布氏族以及科萨部落的古老传说激发了他的想象力，为他指明了真理与谬误的区别。罗利赫拉赫拉聆听年长的牧童们讲述奇异的神话，还心怀敬畏地听那些职业说书人编撰的关于英雄、献身、还有激情的故事。最让罗利赫拉赫拉着迷的，永远是关于远古时期大地上出现的第一批人类的故事。

库奴是个和睦的村落，那里的居民彼此间与其说是邻居，不如说是一个大家庭 。虽然白人很少涉足此地，但是当地的政府代表是白人，而距村子最近的一处商店也同样归白人所有。有时候会有白人旅行者或白人警察路过这个小村庄，不过他们只是稀罕的过客罢了。

[1] edible 可食用的
[2] twine 细绳；麻线
[3] slingshot 弹弓
[4] sparked 激发
[5] chronicled 把……载于编年史中，记载

新的经历

库奴的绝大多数居民都是科萨族人，但另外还有一部分姆丰古人，这个种族是在19世纪早期迁入科萨族领土的。将近100年过去了，姆丰古人在这片土地上仍然和科萨人格格不入。他们的主人时常看不起他们。由于没有自己的土地，他们从一开始就被迫从事没人想干的工作。

Gradually, however, the Mfengu began to pursue European-style education, to master English, and to adopt a western style of dress and housing. They eventually became clergymen, policemen, teachers, and clerks—all relatively well-paid positions. Their success did not make the Mfengu any more popular with the Xhosa. There was some hostility[1], resentment[2], and prejudice between the two groups.

Rolihlahla's father had a different attitude from most of the Xhosa, however. He judged people on their actions rather than on their ethnic origins. He urged his son to do the same, but not just in words. Rolihlahla watched his father form bonds of friendship across ethnic and religious divides. One such friendship, formed with a Mfengu man, would have a profound effect on Rolihlahla's early life.

Ben Mbekela, a retired Mfengu teacher, noticed Rolihlahla's curiosity and intelligence. He told Rolihlahla's parents that their son might have a bright future if he were educated in one of the newly established Methodist schools near the village. Though no one in the family had ever attended school, Rolihlahla's father took to the idea immediately. At age seven, Rolihlahla enrolled in the local Methodist school.

Attending school was quite an adjustment. Rolihlahla stepped into a strange new world that forced him to change the language he spoke and the clothes he wore. Gone was his traditional dress—a piece of cloth

wrapped around his body. In its place, Rolihlahla wore a pair of his father's cutoff[3] pants, a piece of string as a belt, and a western-style shirt. The other students, who came from wealthier families, poked fun at[4] the new student. But Rolihlahla felt no shame. He was proud to wear his father's oversized pants.

Rolihlahla even received a new name. His teacher, Miss Mdingane, politely told

然而，渐渐地，姆丰古人开始接受欧式教育，掌握了英语，还在衣着和居住方面采用了西式风格。他们最终成了当地的牧师、警察、教师和职员——都是相对报酬较高的职位。他们的成功并没有得到科萨人的承认。两个种族间存在着敌对、怨恨与偏见。

不过，罗利赫拉赫拉的父亲在这个问题上与大多数的族人不同。他判断人是以他们的言行为标准，而不是以种族区分。他要求儿子也这样做，但从来不是说说而已。罗利赫拉赫拉亲眼目睹自己的父亲与人建立了跨越种族和宗教信仰的友谊。也正是父亲与一个姆丰古男子的友谊，对罗利赫拉赫拉的早年生活产生了深远的影响。

本·姆贝克拉是一名姆丰古族的退休教师，他注意到了罗利赫拉赫拉的好奇心和聪慧。他对罗利赫拉赫拉的父母说，如果送他们的孩子去离村子不远的新建的循道宗学校接受教育的话，他会有个光明的未来。虽然此前这个家庭里根本没人上过学，但是罗利赫拉赫拉的父亲立即就答应了。于是在7岁时，罗利赫拉赫拉进入了当地的循道宗学校。

上学是个很大的转变。罗利赫拉赫拉进入了一个全新的世界，这里迫使他改变使用的语言和身上的衣着。传统的民族服饰——裹住身体的一块布——不能再用了。取而代之的是，罗利赫拉赫拉套上父亲的一条截短过的裤子，用一根绳子作裤腰带，加上一件西式的衬衫。那些来自富裕家庭的学生嘲笑他们的新同学。但是罗利赫拉赫拉没有丝毫的羞愧。穿上父亲过大的裤子，他感到十分骄傲。

罗利赫拉赫拉甚至有了个新名字。他的老师姆丁贾尼小姐礼貌地告诉他，他的新名字叫纳

[1] hostility 敌意
[2] resentment 怨恨

[3] cutoff （牛仔裤等）截短的，截短后毛边不缝起的
[4] poked fun at 嘲弄，嘲笑

him that his new name was Nelson and that this was the name he would answer to in school. Nobody knows why the teacher chose Nelson. Maybe she was thinking of the British naval captain, Lord Horatio Nelson. There was no way to know for sure. Unlike African names, English names did not come with meanings and tales.

Nelson first assumed he was renamed because Europeans had trouble pronouncing African names. But later he wondered if there had been some other reason. He noticed that African history was absent from his studies and that students were encouraged to think of African ways as backward. He wondered if there was a connection between these ideas and his new English name.

This was a time of wondering and difficult lessons. When Nelson was nine, his father arrived unexpectedly at his mother's home. Mphakanyiswa usually divided his time evenly between the households of his four wives. The schedule was fairly routine[1]. So Nelson and his mother were surprised when Mphakanyiswa showed up several days early. They were also surprised by how sick Mphakanyiswa looked. He had lost weight and coughed violently, almost without stopping. He complained about his lungs. Like many Xhosa people, Mphakanyiswa had a great passion for smoking, and his health problems were likely a result of this habit.

Nelson's mother, with the help of the youngest cowife, did what she could to care for Mphakanyiswa. Nothing could relieve the hacking[2] cough, however—until Mphakanyiswa called for his wife to fetch his tobacco and pipe. The two wives hesitated out of fear that smoking would only make the man's condition worse. Still, Rolihlahla's father insisted, and the wives

尔逊，以后在学校里他就叫这个名字。没人知道为什么老师选了纳尔逊这个名字。也许她想到了英国海军舰长，霍雷肖·纳尔逊勋爵。到底如何已无从考证。与非洲名字不同，英语名字没有什么特定的含义和故事。

纳尔逊一开始认为，之所以自己要被重新命名，是因为欧洲人对非洲人名的发音很头疼。可是后来，他想知道是否还有其他的原因。他注意到自己的课程里没有关于非洲历史的内容，而且学生们被灌输一种思想，认为非洲的东西都是过时的东西。他想知道这些思想与自己的新名字之间是否有着某种联系。

这一时期充满着困惑和各种艰难的课程。纳尔逊9岁时，一天父亲突然不期而至，来到母亲的家里。穆帕卡尼斯瓦平时总是平均分配在4个妻子家里的时间。日程安排也相对固定。所以当穆帕卡尼斯瓦提前几天出现时，母子俩大吃一惊。让他们更吃惊的是穆帕卡尼斯瓦看上去像是生了重病。他消瘦了许多，并不停地拼命咳嗽。他说他的肺出了问题。就像许多科萨人一样，穆帕卡尼斯瓦抽烟非常凶，而他的健康问题可能也是由此导致的。

纳尔逊的母亲与丈夫最小的妻子一起竭尽全力照顾穆帕卡尼斯瓦。可是，任何努力都不能缓解猛烈的干咳——穆帕卡尼斯瓦最后让妻子把他的烟草和烟袋拿来给他。两个妻子担心继续抽烟只能使情况变得更糟，所以犹豫不决。可是罗利赫拉赫拉的父亲仍然固执己见，妻子

[1] routine　日常的，常规的

[2] hacking　短促频繁地干咳

纳尔逊·曼德拉

finally gave in. Mphakanyiswa took a deep draw on the pipe, stopped coughing, and was suddenly calm. For another hour or so, he continued to smoke. Then, with the pipe still lit, he quietly died.

The elders claimed it was a blessing for a man to die so peacefully. But at age nine, Nelson could only grieve[1] the loss of his father. It was his father who had provided him with his sense of identity. His father had defined him. With his father gone, Nelson's life changed drastically[2].

NELSON MANDELA

最后只好妥协。穆帕卡尼斯瓦接过烟袋深吸一口，停止了咳嗽，突然变得很平静。在接下来的大约一个小时里，他继续抽烟。最后，烟筒还燃着，他就平静地死去了。

老人们说，一个人能如此平静地死去是上天的恩赐。可是9岁的纳尔逊感到的只有丧父之痛。是父亲让他认清了自己的身份。父亲界定了他自身的含义。父亲离去了，纳尔逊的生活也发生了翻天覆地的变化。

[1] grieve 为……伤心

[2] drastically 剧烈地；激烈地

纳尔逊·曼德拉

CHAPTER THREE

IN THE ROYAL KRAAL

在王室村庄

Shortly after Mphakanyiswa's funeral, Nelson's mother told him that he was to leave Qunu. The news was something of a shock, but Nelson didn't question her about where he was going or why. African children did not question their elders. Nelson simply packed a few items and prepared to go.

He and his mother started out early in the day. The morning sun gave the village a warm glow. As they climbed a hill overlooking Qunu, Nelson studied the houses, fields, and surrounding forest. He wondered if he would ever see his home again, and he tried hard to burn the scene into his memory. He thought about his friends herding cattle, stick fighting, and playing in the forest. He already missed them.

Nelson and his mother walked all day, mostly in silence. Then, late in the afternoon, they entered a valley that contained a village. In the center was a compound more impressive than anything he'd ever seen. In structure, the buildings reminded Nelson of the huts in his mother's village. But the fine thatched roofs seemed incredibly high. The walls were whitewashed and gleamed[1] in the sun. The buildings had a look of elegance that was unfamiliar to Nelson. Nearby, there were neatly tended gardens, fertile fields, fruit trees, and herds of cattle and sheep.

Nelson's eyes grew wide with wonder as he watched several men step from fine luxury cars that had pulled into the village. Among the group was a stocky[2], dark-skinned man who came toward the two travelers with his hand extended. He was Jongintaba—regent of the Thembu tribe of the Xhosa nation.

Jongintaba! His name meant "one who looks at the mountain." This was the man

穆帕卡尼斯瓦的葬礼结束不久，母亲告诉纳尔逊，他就要离开库奴了。这个消息让人有些吃惊，但纳尔逊没有问母亲他将去何处，为什么要离开。非洲的孩子不能质疑长辈。纳尔逊简单地收拾了几样东西就准备上路了。

他和母亲一早就出门。朝阳把村子照得很温暖。爬上一座俯瞰库奴的小山，纳尔逊最后扫视了一下库奴的屋舍、田园和周围的树林。他想知道自己是否还能再见到家乡，他极力将那景色牢牢印在记忆中。他想到了那些放牛、用棍子比武和在森林里玩耍的朋友们。他已经想他们了。

纳尔逊和母亲一整天都在赶路，彼此几乎没有什么话。最后，快到晚上的时候，他们走进一处山谷，山谷里有个村庄。村子中间有一片复合建筑，它是纳尔逊所见过的最使他印象深刻的建筑。从结构上看，这些建筑让他想起母亲村子里的棚屋。可是这些建筑精致的茅草屋顶显得出奇的高大。墙壁经过粉刷，在阳光下熠熠生辉。这些建筑散发出的那种雅致让纳尔逊感到陌生。房子边上是打理得很整洁的花园、肥沃的土地、结满了果实的树木，还有成群的牛羊。

几辆豪华轿车开进村子，从车上走下几名男子，而这时，纳尔逊已经惊讶得睁大了眼睛。其中一个身材矮壮、皮肤黝黑的男子伸出手朝母子俩走来。这个人就是容欣塔巴——科萨部落坦布氏族的摄政王。

容欣塔巴！这个名字的意思是"眺望山峰的人"。这

[1] gleamed　闪烁；发微光

[2] stocky　矮而壮的

纳尔逊·曼德拉

Nelson's father had supported so many years before—a man who would repay that act with countless acts of kindness. Mother and son were warmly received and together enjoyed the hospitality of the village for a few days—long enough for Nelson to settle in. This was to be his new home.

Nelson missed his mother when she left but quickly adjusted to his new surroundings. Jongintaba and his wife treated Nelson like their own son. He was like a brother to the regent's two children, especially to the regent's son, Justice. He ate with the family, slept in their house, and was respected by visitors.

Nelson's new home was the center of tribal government for the Thembu. The regent called meetings as needed, and discussions focused on issues like drought, caring for cattle, and new laws or policies. All tribal members were welcome, and every man was given the chance to speak, regardless of his station in life. The men talked and argued until everyone agreed.

Nelson attended the meetings and listened carefully. He particularly enjoyed the heated discussions that preceded any decision or action. This was African democracy at work. "Democracy meant all men were to be heard, and a decision was taken together as a people," Nelson would later write in his autobiography. "Majority rule was a foreign notion. A minority was not to be crushed by a majority."

In later years, Nelson would remember what took place in the royal kraal and it would affect his own leadership style. The system had flaws[1], but there was something of value there as well. Watching the process at work sharpened Nelson's interest in history and the ways in which people might work together.

就是许多年前纳尔逊的父亲极力推举的那个人——如今轮到他涌泉相报了。母子俩受到了热情的款待，他们一同享受了好几天村民们的好客之情——直到纳尔逊开始适应了这里的生活。这里将是他的新家。

当母亲离开后，纳尔逊想念她，不过很快就适应了新环境。容欣塔巴夫妇对纳尔逊视如己出。他就像摄政王两个孩子的兄弟一般，尤其与摄政王的儿子贾斯帝斯更显亲密。他和全家人一起吃饭，睡在他们的房间里，也同样受到来访者的尊敬。

纳尔逊的新家是坦布氏族政府的核心。必要时，摄政王在此召集会议，议题主要集中在干旱、照看家畜，以及制定新的法律或政策等问题上。所有的部落成员都可以参加这样的会议，无论什么身份，与会者都有发言的机会。所有人各抒己见，互相争论，直到所有人都达成一致。

纳尔逊参加这些会议，认真聆听。他对最终得出一致决议的激烈辩论特别感兴趣。这是正在实行的非洲民主。"民主的含义就是每个人都会被聆听，进而得出令所有人都信服的决议，"纳尔逊后来在自传中如是写道。"少数服从多数原则是个外来概念。少数人不应该成为多数人的牺牲品。"

时过境迁，纳尔逊对于发生在王室村庄中的故事仍记忆犹新，这一切将会对他自己的领导风格产生影响。这种制度存在弊病，但是有一定的价值。旁观这一制度的运作，激发了纳尔逊对历史的兴趣，同时也使他想了解人们如何可以进行协作。

[1] flaws　缺陷；瑕疵

Visiting chiefs fascinated Nelson. Many were wise and well spoken. Nelson was particularly impressed by an elderly man named Chief Zwelibhangile Joyi. The chief loved to tell stories about the heroes of the past. Although old and quite wrinkled[1], he seemed to swell[2] with youthful power when he recalled the courage of the Xhosa warriors who stood against the powerful nineteenth-century British army. The chief also talked about the ancient ancestors of the Xhosa who had lived in the great lakes region of east-central Africa. Nelson loved to sit and listen to these tales.

Stepping Stones to Manhood

Without Nelson realizing it, he was being groomed[3] to fill a role his father had held before him—adviser to the king. By the time he was sixteen, Nelson had become an impressive young man. But he was not yet an adult in the traditional or tribal sense. The rite[4] of circumcision[5] would make him an adult in the eyes of the community.

Circumcision, the cutting of a young man's foreskin, is a minor operation. But more important than the actual procedure was the transmission of Xhosa values and the sense of group unity. Leading up to the operation and during the period of recovery, boys received instruction on what it meant to be an adult in Xhosa society. A similar ceremony took place for girls, but without any physical operation.

Following the circumcision, Nelson and other young men his age rested in secluded[6] huts until their wounds properly healed. Afterward, the huts were burned to the ground with all the contents inside. The boys' last links to childhood were destroyed, and they were considered men. According to

纳尔逊对于来拜访的各位首领非常着迷。许多首领很有智慧，也能言善辩。纳尔逊尤其对一位叫兹韦立班纪利·兆伊的年长首领印象深刻。这位首领喜欢讲历史英雄的故事。他虽然已经老得满脸皱纹，可是每当讲起关于科萨勇士们如何抗击19世纪强大的英国军队的故事时，体内似乎充满了年轻的力量。这位首领还喜欢讲古代科萨人在非洲中东部大湖区的生活。纳尔逊喜欢坐着听这些故事。

成长的阶石

纳尔逊没有意识到，他自己正在为接过父亲的衣钵——成为首领智囊——而接受训练。到了16岁时，纳尔逊已经是个让人不能小觑的青年了。不过从传统或部落习俗的角度来说，他还不是成年人。只有经过割礼仪式，族人才会正式把他看做成年人。

割礼——就是割除年轻男子的包皮——只是个小手术。不过，比具体仪式更重要的是对于科萨价值观与种族团结意识的传承。在进行手术前以及康复的过程中，男孩将接受教育，让他们知道作为成年科萨人的含义。女孩也有一个类似的仪式，但是没有手术。

割礼过后，纳尔逊和其他几个参加割礼的年轻人在隔离的茅屋里休息，直到伤口愈合。然后，这些茅屋以及里面的物品会一起被烧掉。这些男孩与童年时期最后的联系被毁灭了，从此，他们将被当成男人看待。根

[1] wrinkled 有皱纹的

[2] swell 被充满

[3] groomed 使作好准备，训练

[4] rite 仪式

[5] circumcision 割礼

[6] secluded 隔离的；偏僻的

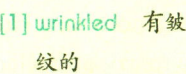

纳尔逊·曼德拉

tradition, Nelson also received a circumcision name. It was Dalibunga, which roughly translated means "the founder of the rulers of the Transkei."

Finally, with great fanfare[1], Nelson and the other young men were presented to the tribe as full-fledged[2] members. The ceremony was like a high school graduation, a cotillion[3], and a birthday party all rolled into one. Villagers watched as the young men were presented to society. Proud parents showered their children with gifts[4], and Nelson was as proud as anyone to take his place in the adult world of his people.

Among the many people who spoke that day was a man named Chief Meligqili. He stood and surveyed the throng[5] that had gathered. Then he looked at the young men and started to speak:

There sit our sons; young, healthy, and handsome, the flower of the Xhosa tribe, the pride of our nation. We have just circumcised them in a ritual that promises them manhood, but I am here to tell you that it is an empty, illusory[6] promise, a promise that can never be fulfilled. For we Xhosas, and all black South Africans are a conquered people.

Suddenly, the mood shifted. What had started as a purely joyous occasion turned somber[7]. Smiles fell away from the faces of parents and children alike. They clearly did not want to hear this kind of talk, but the old man pressed on:

We are slaves in our own country. We are tenants[8] on our own soil.

We have no strength, no power, no control over our own destiny in the land of our birth. [The young men] will go to cities where they will live in shacks[9] and drink cheap alcohol all because we have no land to give them where they could prosper and multiply. They will cough their lungs out deep in the bowels of the white man's mines, destroying their health, never seeing the sun, so that the white

据传统，纳尔逊有了割礼名字。名字是达利本贾，大概意思是"特兰斯凯统治者的创始人"。

最后，在响亮的短曲中，纳尔逊和其他青年在族人面前作为成年人被介绍一番。这一仪式有点像是把高中毕业典礼、大型正式舞会以及生日派对合而为一的庆祝活动。村民们共同见证年轻人被介绍进入社交界。骄傲的父母们为孩子准备了大量礼物，纳尔逊和每个族人一样，为自己成为部落中的成年人而感到无比自豪。

那一天的仪式上有许多人发言，其中有个首领叫梅利齐利。他站起来环顾了一下人群。然后看着几个年轻人，说：

在座的是我们的孩子；年轻，健壮，帅气，是科萨的花朵，部落的骄傲。我们刚刚为他们行了割礼，承认他们的成人地位，可是，我在这里要告诉你们，这种承认是空虚的，虚假的，永远无法兑现的。因为我们科萨人，以及南非的所有黑人都是亡国奴。

突然间，气氛改变了。纯粹的快乐气氛被阴郁所取代。父母们和子女们脸上的笑容消失了。很明显，他们不愿听到这样的话语，可是老人继续着：

我们在自己的国家里沦为奴隶。我们在自己的土地上成了租户。在我们生长的地方，我们没有力量，没有权力，无法决定自己的命运。（这些年轻人）将要到城市去，他们将住在陋室中，喝廉价的酒，就因为我们没法给他们土地，让他们可以自我发展，繁衍后代。他们将在白人拥有的深深的矿井里把整个肺咳坏，把健康摧毁，永远不见天日，就为了让那些白人

纳尔逊·曼德拉

[1] fanfare （通常用小号吹奏的用以宣告节庆开始或要人到场的）礼节性响亮短曲

[2] full-fledged 成熟的

[3] cotillion 大型正式舞会

[4] showered ... with gifts 送某人大量礼物

[5] throng 群，群众

[6] illusory 幻觉的；虚假的

[7] somber 阴郁的

[8] tenants 佃户

[9] shacks 简陋的房屋

man can live a life of unequaled prosperity. Among these young men are chiefs who will never rule because we have no power to govern ourselves; soldiers who will never fight for we have no weapons to fight with; scholars who will never teach because we have no place for them to study. The abilities, intelligence, the promise of these young men will be squandered[1] in their attempt to eke out a living[2] doing the simplest, most mindless chores for the white man. The gifts today are for naught[3], for we cannot give them the greatest gift of all, which is freedom and independence.

As the words washed over Nelson, he felt an intense anger toward the speaker. This was to have been one of the happiest days of his life, and this man had ruined it with his ranting[4]. Nelson wished those foul words had never been spoken, and tried to flush them from his mind. But the words had seeped[5] into his soul, where they began to work on him.

Nelson would later look back on that ceremony and realize that his childhood had ended then not only in a physical and social fashion. His childish notions about the political world were also beginning to fall away.

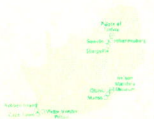

可以过上不平等的奢侈生活。这些年轻人中，有的是永远不能发号施令的首领，因为我们根本没有支配自己的权力；有的是永远不能战斗的士兵，因为我们根本没有打仗的武器；有的是永远不能站上讲台的学者，因为我们根本没有让他们学习的地方。这些年轻人的能力、聪明才智和前途因生存所迫而全部浪掷于为白人服务的、最简单、最没有意义的杂役中。今天我们给的礼物一无用处，只因我们没法给他们最伟大的礼物，那就是自由与独立。

当这些话语劈头盖脸地涌来时，纳尔逊对演讲者怒不可遏。这本该是他一生中最快乐的一天，可是这个人却用一阵大叫大嚷毁掉了他的快乐。纳尔逊希望那些肮脏的话语从来没有被说出，他努力将这些话从脑海里摒除掉。可是，那些话已经渗入了他的灵魂，在那里它们开始对他产生了影响。

之后，纳尔逊再次回顾那次仪式，他明白从那一刻起，他的童年已不仅从生理上或社会关系上结束了。他对于政治世界的幼稚看法也开始消失。

[1] squandered
浪费

[2] eke out a living
竭力维持生计；
勉强度日

[3] naught　无；零

[4] ranting　大叫
大嚷

[5] seeped　渗
漏；（观念等）
渗入

纳尔逊·曼德拉

CHAPTER FOUR

GOING TO SCHOOL

进入学校

A t age sixteen, Nelson continued his formal education. That was something of a luxury for African children, who often received only a few years of schooling before taking menial[1] jobs. But Mandela was not destined for working in the mines or a white farmer's field. He was to be the advisor to kings.

He enrolled in Clarkebury Boarding Institute, one of the best schools for black youths in southern Africa. Children from many of the region's prominent families attended. They were often well educated and sophisticated. As the regent's ward, Nelson was used to getting respect. He quickly discovered that he no longer stood out, however. Nearly everyone in his school had prestige in their home villages.

Although he thought of himself as nearly grown when he left home, Nelson realized that he was something of a yokel[2]. He lost confidence in himself and tried to fit in with the more refined students. In the end, however, he learned it was best to be himself. Ability in his schoolwork was ultimately what mattered most.

All and all, his time at the school was a good experience that laid a firm foundation for future studies. More than anything, he learned that the world was a much bigger place than he had imagined. He carried that feeling with him when he graduated from Clarkebury and went on to a school named Healdtown, located in Fort Beaufort.

The school was built on the site of a nineteenth-century British fort that had served as an important outpost during the war against the Xhosa. But by the time Nelson arrived there in 1937, there were no open signs of war. The cluster of structures that

NELSON MANDELA

[1] menial 仆役
工作的

[2] yokel 乡巴佬

在 16 岁时，纳尔逊继续接受正规教育。这对于非洲孩子来说是一种奢侈，他们通常都是只接受几年教育，之后就开始从事仆人的工作。可是曼德拉的命运不是让他在矿井里或者是白人农场里工作。他注定要成为首领智囊。

他进入克拉克伯里寄宿学校读书，这所学校是非洲南部最好的黑人学校之一。这个地区的许多望族子弟都来这里读书。他们往往都受过好的教育，老于世故。从前，在摄政王的保护下，纳尔逊习惯了受人尊敬。他很快发现，现在他已经没有什么突出的身份了。几乎这里的每个人在他们自己的家乡都享有声望。

虽然在离开家的时候他感觉自己已经长大了，可是在这里，纳尔逊感觉自己有点像乡巴佬。他对自己失去了信心，想方设法融入这些高雅的同学。然而到了最后，他发现做自己才是最好的。优异的成绩才是最重要的。

总而言之，在学校的经历是有益的，并为他以后的学习打下了坚实的基础。最重要的是，他明白了世界远比他想像的要大得多。他带着这样的想法从克拉克伯里毕业，之后进入位于博福特堡的希尔特敦学校。

这所学校建在一座 19 世纪英国堡垒的旧址上，这个堡垒在英国和科萨的战争中是一处重要的前哨。但是，当纳尔逊在 1937 年来到这里时，已经没有了明显的战争迹象。成群的建

纳尔逊·曼德拉

formed the campus overlooked a beautiful valley. The buildings were covered with ivy, and tree-lined paths crisscrossed between them. Healdtown was a coed[1] institution with more than a thousand black students.

Healdtown's principal, Dr. Arthur Wellington, was a proud descendant of the Duke of Wellington, a famous English general. Dr. Wellington was very British and thought that the world needed more Englishmen. He set about producing black Englishmen at the school. "We were taught—and believed—that the best ideas were English ideas, the best government was English government, and the best men were Englishmen," Nelson later said.

Though the school was more tolerant than some other European institutions, the instructors still made the same assumption—that Africans were backward. This attitude helped to create a sense of inferiority on the part of the students.

Even with its flaws, Healdtown did produce disciplined scholars. Students were up at 6:00 A.M. and continued their academic day until 5:00 P.M. They were expected to be in their rooms by 9:30 P.M., and their weekday evenings consisted of dinner, an hour break, and two hours of study hall. This was a rigorous schedule, but it did a lot to develop the mental muscles of the students.

The college, which was comparable to a high school in the American system, attracted students from many different parts of South Africa. Nelson met people from Basutoland, Swaziland, and Bechuanaland. There was friction between the Xhosa and other tribes. Even with his father's example, Mandela still carried some negative feelings about other ethnic groups.

筑组成了校园，与远处美丽的山谷遥相呼应。建筑上爬满了常春藤，林荫小道贯穿其间。希尔特敦是一所男女同校的学院，有超过1 000名黑人学生。

希尔特敦的校长亚瑟·威灵顿博士是英国著名将军威灵顿公爵的后嗣，为人傲慢。他是个典型的英国人，认为世界需要更多的英国人。他办学的目标就是培养黑皮肤的英国人。"我们被灌输——并以为——最好的思想是英国思想，最好的政府是英国政府，最好的人是英国人，"纳尔逊后来说道。

虽然这所学校已经比其他一些欧洲学院要宽容不少，学校的教师仍然抱着相同的观念——非洲人就是落后的。这种态度使得学生感到自己低人一等。

尽管存在弊端，希尔特敦还是培养了不少训练有素的学者。学生们早晨6点起床，一直到下午5点才结束一天的学习。晚上9点半就寝，平日的晚间内容包括晚餐、一小时的休息，还有两小时的自习时间。这一作息表很严格，然而对于开发学生的智力也助益良多。

公学，也就是美国教育体系中的高中，吸引了来自南非不同地区的学生。纳尔逊遇到了来自巴苏陀兰、斯威士兰和贝专纳的学生。科萨与其他部落存在摩擦。即便有了父亲的榜样，曼德拉对其他种族仍然有些心存抵触。

[1]coed 男女同校的

纳尔逊·曼德拉

Nelson did well in school. He also participated in athletics and became a good long-distance runner on the track team. In his second year, Mandela took up boxing. It was the start of a lifelong passion.

In his final year, Nelson became a prefect[1], an honor bestowed[2] on students who excelled in academics or showed leadership abilities. He was proud of this accomplishment. Still, the high point of the year came later, toward the end of the term, when the school was visited by Samuel Krune Mqhayi. Mqhayi was a poet who had written part of the South African national anthem, *Nkosi Sikelel' iAfrika*. The first verse and chorus of the song had been written in 1897 by Enoch Sontonga, a Xhosa teacher. In 1927, Mqhayi added seven more verses.

When Mqhayi spoke at Nelson's school, his words shocked the students. "We cannot allow these foreigners who do not care for our culture to take over our nation," Mqhayi warned. "I predict that one day, the forces of African society will achieve a momentous victory."

The words awakened something in Nelson. They made him think of the regent's royal kraal, the heroes brought to life by Chief Joyi's tales, even the disturbing words spoken at the circumcision rites. The words were magical. When the poet moved, all eyes followed. The students' spirits rose and fell to the sound of Mqhayi's voice.

When the poet finished speaking, the students stood with thunderous applause. Nelson felt himself touched in a deep way. Like many students, he had come to doubt the ability of Africans to compete with Europeans. But Mqhayi made Nelson remember the great power of his own roots. He had never felt any prouder to be Xhosa than at that moment. It was his first step

NELSON MANDELA

纳尔逊在学校里表现很好。他还参加了体育比赛，在田径队里是个长跑好手。到了第二年，曼德拉开始接触拳击。那也是他毕生爱好的开始。

在最后一年里，纳尔逊成为班长，只有成绩优秀或展现出领导才能的学生才可以获得这项荣誉。他为自己所取得的成绩感到自豪。然而，这一年的高潮还没有来临，到了学期快结束的时候，塞缪尔·科鲁尼·姆克哈伊前来学校访问。姆克哈伊是一名诗人，他是南非国歌《佑我南非》部分歌词的作者。这首歌的第一段诗文以及合唱部分是由科萨教师英纳科·宋东加于1897年撰写的。在1927年，姆克哈伊给歌曲增加了7段诗文。

姆克哈伊在学校里演讲时，他的话让学生们非常震惊。"我们不能让这些外国人，这些对我们的文明漠不关心的外国人，占领我们的国家，"姆克哈伊警告说。"我预言，终会有一天，非洲社会的力量将取得历史性的胜利。"

这些话唤醒了纳尔逊体内的某种东西。这些话让他想起了摄政王的王室村庄，兆伊首领的故事中那些栩栩如生的英雄，甚至割礼仪式上的那个扫兴的演讲。这些话具有某种魔力。当姆克哈伊走动时，所有的眼睛都跟着他。所有学生的心情随着姆克哈伊的嗓音而高低起伏。

当诗人结束讲话时，学生们起立报以雷鸣般的掌声。纳尔逊觉得自己被深深地打动了。像许多学生一样，他对于非洲人民是否有能力与欧洲列强竞争表示怀疑。但是姆克哈伊使纳尔逊追忆起自己民族所具有的强大的生命力。他从没有像那一刻那样为自己是科萨族的一员而感到骄傲。

[1] prefect （尤指英国公学中有权维持纪律的）级长，班长

[2] bestowed 将……授予；赠予

toward becoming a freedom fighter.

Higher Learning

In 1940, as World War II raged in Europe, twenty-one-year-old Nelson Mandela began his first year at the all-black University College of Fort Hare. He arrived in a sleek[1], double-breasted gray suit, a gift from Jongintaba. The school was a small, highly regarded college patterned after Oxford in England. There were only 150 students, and they were among the brightest in southern Africa.

Nelson had long dreamed of this day. He believed education was the key to success in the modern world, and Fort Hare was the finest institution available to a Xhosa man of his era. Since a number of other students had been his schoolmates before, he felt at home there. Many students were new to him, but they seemed to be kindred[2] spirits. Among them was Oliver Tambo, who was destined to become a lifelong friend and partner of Nelson's. He also met some of the greatest minds on the African continent at that time. He studied with such outstanding African professors as Z. K. Matthews and D. D. T. Jabavu.

From the start, Nelson planned to study law, in preparation for his role as tribal advisor. In his first year, his studies included Roman Dutch law and Native Administration—a class that focused on laws affecting

Africans. Many of these laws were intended to keep blacks and whites apart.

At the time, Nelson believed race relations were getting better in his country. World War II had something to do with his sentiment[3]. During the war, South Africa fought against the racism of Nazi Germany. Nelson and other black thinkers assumed it was just a matter of time before South

那是他向成为一名自由战士迈出的第一步。

高等教育

1940 年，当第二次世界大战在欧洲打响时，21 岁的纳尔逊·曼德拉开始了他在全黑人大学福特海尔大学的第一年学习生活。他去学校时穿着一件面料光滑、双排扣的灰色上衣，这是容欣塔巴给他的礼物。这所学校规模很小，口碑非常好，学校仿照英国牛津大学的模式。这里只有 150 名学生，都是非洲南部最聪明的人。

纳尔逊对于这一天已经梦想很久了。他相信，教育是在现代世界中取得成功的关键，而福特海尔是他那个年代里一个科萨人能企及的最好的学校。由于许多同学也是他从前的校友，纳尔逊在那里感觉很自在。许多学生对他来说是陌生的，不过他们似乎都与他有着共同的志向。其中就包括奥利弗·坦博，这个人注定将成为纳尔逊一生的朋友与搭档。在那一时期里，他还遇到一些非洲大陆上最卓越的智者。他师从许多杰出的非洲教授，比如马修斯和贾巴武。

一开始，纳尔逊计划攻读法律，为他以后成为部落智囊做准备。第一年，他的课程包括"罗马荷兰法与黑人管理"——这门课的内容主要是关于对非洲人产生影响的法律。这些法律中的相当一部分都倾向于将黑人与白人隔离。

在那时，纳尔逊相信在他的国家内，各种族之间的关系正在逐渐好转。第二次世界大战对他的观点产生了某种影响。战争期间，南非与纳粹德国的种族主义作斗争。纳尔逊和其他黑人思想家认为，南非人民在自己的国家里开展反种族主

[1] sleek 光滑的

[2] kindred 同类的；同性质的

[3] sentiment 观点

纳尔逊·曼德拉

• 53

Africans would fight against racism at home, too.

But when Nelson met fellow students Nyathi Khongisa and Paul Mahabane, he began to change his mind. Khongisa and Mahabane had reputations as rebels, and they introduced Nelson to the African National Congress (ANC). Nelson had heard of the organization but knew little about it.

He learned that the ANC had been established in 1912 to work for racial equality in South Africa. Its members were mostly middle-class urban blacks and royal members of tribal society. The group had a lot in common with the National Association for the Advancement of Colored People (NAACP), established around the same time in the United States. It stressed peaceful protest, dialogue between whites and blacks, and education about the plight[1] of black South Africans.

Exposure to the ANC changed the way Nelson thought about himself. He stopped looking at himself as simply a Xhosa man and began to see himself as an African. The ANC helped turn him into an activist who was ready to do battle against injustice where and when he saw it.

His new attitude eventually brought him into conflict with the school administration. Fort Hare students wanted a stronger voice in the running of their school, and to protest, Nelson and several others launched a boycott[2] of student government elections. That boycott resulted in the students' expulsion[3] from school.

Country Boy, City Man

The ride back to the royal kraal was a troubling one. Nelson knew that Jongintaba would be displeased with his expulsion. Jongintaba expected Nelson to complete his

义斗争只是个时间问题。

但是，当纳尔逊结识了他的同学尼亚西·鸿基萨和保罗·马哈班额后，他的想法改变了。鸿基萨和马哈班额都是著名的"叛乱分子"，他们将纳尔逊介绍给非洲人国民大会（非国大）。纳尔逊从前只是听说过该组织，对其知之甚少。

他了解到非国大成立于 1912 年，致力于南非的种族平等事业。其成员大多是城市黑人中的中产阶级以及部落的王族。这个组织与同一时期在美国成立的全国有色人种促进协会有许多共同之处。它强调采取和平手段进行抗议、开展白人与黑人间的对话、将南非黑人的悲惨境地作为教育内容。

受到非国大的影响，纳尔逊改变了对自身的认识。他不再认为自己只是一个科萨人，而是开始将自己视为一个非洲人。非国大帮助他转变为一个激进主义分子，使他随时随地准备向面临的不平等宣战。

他的新态度最终使他陷入与学校当局的冲突中。福特海尔的学生希望在管理学校事务的问题上有更多发言权，为了表示抗议，纳尔逊与其他一些学生联合抵制学生会的选举。这次抵制活动最终导致参与其中的学生被学校开除。

乡下男孩，城市男人

在回王室村庄的路上，纳尔逊感到很苦恼，他知道容欣塔巴对他被开除这件事一定很生气。容欣塔巴希望纳尔逊能完成学

[1] plight　困境

[2] boycott　联合抵制

[3] expulsion　驱逐，开除

纳尔逊·曼德拉

degree and become an advisor to the tribal king. Nelson did not look forward to explaining his expulsion to the older man. He approached his home like a condemned[1] man, torn between the desire to stall and the desire to be done with the confrontation[2] as quickly as possible.

During the initial meeting, Jongintaba did not shout. He didn't have to. With a tone of authority Nelson found difficult to resist, Jongintaba simply ordered him to do what was necessary to resume his education. There was no sense in arguing, so Nelson simply agreed and left the matter alone for the time being[3].

Despite the early unpleasantness, things returned to normal for Nelson at the royal kraal. He ran errands[4] for Jongintaba and looked after some of his affairs. It was life as he had known it since he left his mother's home at age nine. The dress, conversations, and schedules were the same. Yet, Nelson saw life much differently. He realized that he had changed. He was no longer the country boy who had left for school years before.

Shortly after Nelson's return, Jongintaba announced that he was getting old and needed to put his affairs in order. At the top of his list was the well-being of his son, Justice, and his ward, Nelson. As part of his plan, Jongintaba had even chosen a wife for Nelson and had already made arrangements for the wedding.

Nelson was horrified. He knew the young woman who had been chosen. She was pleasant enough, but Nelson did not love her. More to the point, he was not ready to settle down. There was too much of the world left to explore. Nelson had been raised to respect his elders, but he was not willing to accept an arranged marriage. He considered himself a modern African man and an arranged

业，继而成为部落首领的智囊。纳尔逊不指望把被开除的事向前辈们解释清楚。他像个罪人一样踏上归途，内心被矛盾煎熬着，一方面想停下脚步，另一方面又希望快点面对这一切，好让它们早点过去。

刚一见面，容欣塔巴没有大吼。他不需要那样做。容欣塔巴那威严的语调令曼德拉很难反抗，他只是命令他做一些必要的事情以继续学业。争辩没有意义，所以纳尔逊就答应了，并把这件事暂时放在一边。

虽然一开始有些不快，但纳尔逊在王室村庄的生活恢复了正常。他为容欣塔巴跑腿，并照料一些事务。从9岁时离开母亲家起，他过的就是这样的生活。服装、谈话和时间安排还是老样子。然而，纳尔逊对生活的看法和从前大不相同。他意识到自己已经改变。他已经不是几年前离开这里去上学的那个乡下男孩了。

纳尔逊回来不久，容欣塔巴宣布，随着自己慢慢变老，他需要定夺一些事情。最首要的问题就是他的儿子贾斯蒂斯和受监护人纳尔逊的幸福问题。作为他计划的一部分，容欣塔巴甚至为纳尔逊选好了一位妻子，婚礼的筹备工作也已经就绪。

纳尔逊感到惊恐。他认识那位被选中的姑娘。她很讨人喜欢，可纳尔逊并不爱她。更重要的是，他还没有做好安家的准备。这个世界还有太多的东西等着他去探索。纳尔逊自幼接受的教育告诉他要尊重长者，但是他不愿接受包办婚姻。他认为自己是个现代的非洲人，而包办

纳尔逊·曼德拉

[1] condemned
被判罪的

[2] confrontation
（对困难境地、
令人不愉快局
面等的）正视，
勇敢面对

[3] for the time be-
ing 暂时

[4] errands 差
事；跑腿

marriage was not a modern idea. He took the only other path available to him—or so it seemed at the time—and that was to run.

Nelson did not only run away from something he disliked. He also ran toward his destiny—to a place called Johannesburg.

婚姻绝不符合现代的观念。他选择了唯一的出路——或者说是那时唯一的出路——那就是逃跑。

纳尔逊不仅逃离了他不喜欢的东西。他也逃向了一个命中注定的地方——一个叫约翰内斯堡的地方。

纳尔逊·曼德拉

CHAPTER FIVE

JOHANNESBURG

约翰内斯堡

A wave of people moved into Johannesburg and other South African cities in the early 1940s. There were few jobs in the black villages, so young blacks, especially men, headed to the cities and surrounding mines. Nelson Mandela was one of them.

Johannesburg was big and crowded, and Nelson's head craned[1] this way and that to take in all the tall buildings. He dodged[2] traffic and navigated the dangers of big city nights. Many things shocked him, but none more than the great difference between the lives of whites and blacks.

Rich white suburbs, scattered throughout the city, were a world apart from the shantytowns[3], or townships[4], to which black people were restricted. The shantytowns were overcrowded, unsanitary, and lacking electricity, tarred[5] roads, or telephones. Violence and family breakdowns were common, but no more common than police raids. Seeing these towns gave Mandela a sort of education he had not found at the schools of his youth.

Mandela needed work, and his best bet seemed to be in the mines. South Africa had huge deposits of coal, gold, and diamonds, and the mines employed many blacks. Mandela took a job as a security guard at a large gold mine. It was a good job compared with working a mile

underground, where cave-ins were a constant threat and miners faced health risks from breathing dust from the digging operations.

He moved into the sprawling[6] black shantytown of Alexandria. Though the shantytown was poor, the energy of the place was something Mandela would remember fondly for decades. He was amazed by his people's ability to find happiness and

在20世纪40年代早期，大量人口涌进约翰内斯堡以及南非的其他城市。在黑人聚居的乡下，就业机会少得可怜，所以年轻的黑人，尤其是男子，纷纷涌向城市以及城市周边的矿区。纳尔逊·曼德拉就是其中之一。

约翰内斯堡很大，很拥挤，纳尔逊伸长脖子，对着高楼大厦上下张望。他在车流中东躲西闪，在城市危机四伏的夜里穿行。许多事情都让他感到震惊，但其中最令他感到震惊的是白人与黑人间生活的天壤之别。

富裕的白人郊区分散在城市的各个地方，与黑人生活的贫民窟天差地远。贫民窟异常拥挤，卫生条件十分糟糕，没有电，没有一条柏油马路，没有一部电话。暴力以及家庭破裂司空见惯，而更加司空见惯的是警察的肆意搜捕。目睹这些城镇使曼德拉受到了一种早年在学校里没有受到过的教育。

曼德拉需要工作，而他最大的机会似乎是在矿井里。南非的煤炭、黄金和钻石的储量非常巨大，各个矿井都雇用了大量的黑人。曼德拉在一个大型金矿找到了一份保安的工作。与在地下一英里的井里工作比起来，他的工作算是不错了，在矿井里，矿工们时刻受到塌方的威胁，而且因为吸入开掘时产生的粉尘，健康也受到严重危害。

他搬进亚历山大区内的一处杂乱无章的黑人贫民窟。虽然贫民窟里非常贫穷，不过它所蕴含的活力却给曼德拉留下了美好的回忆，这些回忆一直保持了几十年。那里的居民在贫穷与肮脏的环境中仍然能找到快乐与尊严，这着实让曼德拉

[1] craned 伸长脖子；探头

[2] dodged 闪躲

[3] shantytowns 贫民区

[4] townships （南非）黑人（或有色人种）居住区

[5] tarred 涂有焦油（或柏油）的

[6] sprawling （城市等）无计划地扩展（或延伸）

纳尔逊·曼德拉

dignity in the midst of poverty and squalor[1].

New Teachers

Alexandria was a magnet that attracted all sorts of black people. Some were criminals. Most were poor people just trying to survive. A few were caring leaders who had the welfare of their people at heart. Among this last group was a man who would have a powerful influence on Mandela. That man was Walter Sisulu.

Like Mandela, Sisulu came from the Transkei region. He was several years older than Mandela and had also worked in the mines. He was one of the lucky few who had moved on to a better job. He had become a real estate agent who handled the few parcels of land still available to blacks in Johannesburg.

Mandela impressed Sisulu from the start. The older man offered Mandela a job with a modest salary and commission. In taking the job, Mandela also shared his plans—to complete his bachelor's degree and to become a lawyer.

South Africa was a hard place for blacks to live and an even harder place for blacks to develop professional skills. Sisulu knew how valuable an education would be to Mandela. He was like a father to the younger man and supported his efforts to finish his degree through correspondence courses[2].

Sisulu also introduced Mandela to the law firm of Witkin, Sidelsky and Eidelman. It was one of the largest firms in Johannesburg and handled many real estate deals involving blacks. The firm was considered liberal, although that did not stop it from charging much higher rates to black clients than to white ones. Still, the firm was willing to hire

[1] squalor　肮脏

惊讶不已。

新的老师

亚历山大区像一块磁石，吸引着形形色色的黑人。其中有些人是罪犯，大部分人只是在努力活下去。另外还有一小部分人是心怀民众疾苦的关心他人的领袖。这些人中就包括一位后来对曼德拉产生深远影响的人。这个人就是瓦尔特·西苏卢。

和曼德拉一样，西苏卢也来自特兰斯凯地区。他比曼德拉年长几岁，开始也在矿里干活。他是为数不多的幸运儿之一，因为之后他得到了一份更好的工作。他当上了地产代理人，手里掌握着约翰内斯堡地区为数不多的几块可以卖给黑人的地产。

曼德拉从一开始就给西苏卢留下了深刻的印象。他给了曼德拉一份工作，薪水和佣金都不太高。曼德拉一边工作一边继续自己的计划——获得学士学位并成为一名律师。

对于黑人来说，想在南非生存已很艰难，想要获得某种专业技能就更是难上加难了。西苏卢很清楚，教育对于曼德拉来说有多么重要。他像父亲一样对待这个比自己小几岁的年轻人，帮助他通过函授课程获得了学位。

[2] correspondence
　　courses　函授
　　课程

西苏卢还将曼德拉介绍到威特金、希德尔斯基和埃德尔曼的律师事务所。那是当时约翰内斯堡最大的事务所之一，负责操作许多涉及黑人的地产买卖。虽然这家事务所给黑人主顾的开价要远远高于白人，不过它还算是开明的。而且，这家事务所愿意雇用

纳尔逊·曼德拉

a black clerk who was working on his degree. Many other firms would not hire a black under any circumstances.

For good reason, Mandela was very excited. On his first day at work, he met most of the staff. They welcomed him and treated him with more respect than whites usually gave blacks. Mandela was particularly impressed with Lazar Sidelsky, a partner in the firm. He seemed genuinely concerned with the plight of black Africans.

Sidelsky thought education was the key to black progress in South Africa. He felt that an educated man like Mandela could do much to uplift the whole race. At the very least, successful black people would provide role models for others, Sidelsky thought. He was quick to point out that Mandela had the potential to be such a role model.

At first Mandela agreed with that point of view, but he later changed his mind. When he got to know another staff member some days later, he realized that a few successful black professionals would not make much difference in the big picture of racial injustice.

Gaur Radebe, the other black clerk in the firm, had been away on business during Mandela's first day. He did, however, seek out[1] the new man upon his return. Radebe was a stocky Zulu man, about ten years older than Mandela. He knew three languages, English, Sotho, and his native Zulu, and he expressed himself well in all of them.

Radebe was also a proud, capable man who spoke his mind freely. He believed he was equal to any man and encouraged Mandela to think the same. While Sidelsky and the other partners taught Mandela the fine points of the law, it was Radebe who taught him the facts of life. "You people stole our land from us and enslaved us," Radebe once said to some white staff members gathered

一名正在攻读学位的黑人职员。其他的许多事务所是无论如何也不会雇用黑人的。

曼德拉当然有理由感到兴奋。第一天上班，他见到了大多数的职员。他们对他表示欢迎，给予他的尊重比通常白人给予黑人的尊重都要多。曼德拉尤其对事务所的合伙人之一——拉扎尔·希德尔斯基印象深刻。他似乎是真心实意地关心非洲黑人所面临的困境。

希德尔斯基认为，教育是南非黑人进步的关键。他觉得像曼德拉这种受过教育的人，对提升整个种族的实力大有好处。至少成功的黑人将给其他人树立典范，希德尔斯基这样想。他立即指出，曼德拉就有成为这种典范的潜质。

一开始，曼德拉对于这种观点表示赞同，不过后来他的想法改变了。几天后当他结识了另一名员工，他发现几个成功的黑人专业人员没法改变种族歧视的大环境。

[1] seek out　找出

高尔·拉德贝是事务所里的另一名黑人雇员，曼德拉刚来的时候他正好出差了。然而他一回来就去见他的新同事。拉德贝是个矮壮的祖鲁人，比曼德拉大10岁左右。他懂3种语言——英语、梭托语，还有他的母语祖鲁语，而且3种语言他都能运用自如。

拉德贝也是个自豪的、有才干的人，总是直抒己见。他相信自己和任何人都是平等的，并鼓励曼德拉也建立这样的信念。如果说希德尔斯基和其他同事教了曼德拉许多有用的法律知识，那么拉德贝则把生活的真相揭示在了曼德拉面前。"你们的人抢走 我们的土地，奴役我们的人民，"拉德贝在一次几个白人职员的非正式聚会上对他

informally. "Now you make us pay through the nose[1] to get the worst pieces of it back."

Mandela discovered just how true those words were. Despite little actual work on the real estate sales, law firms routinely got most of the profits while the black agents received mere crumbs[2]. His own firm, in working with Sisulu's real estate company, always took the lion's share of commissions made on the properties.

On one occasion, Mandela returned to Sidelsky's office after running some errands. Radebe was there. He looked at the younger clerk thoughtfully then turned to Sidelsky, who was seated behind the desk. "Look, you sit there like a lord whilst my chief [Mandela] runs around doing errands for you," he said. "The situation should be reversed, and one day it will, and we will dump all of you into the sea."

Mandela was shocked by the boldness of the statement, but Sidelsky simply shook his head and did not respond. Later he told Mandela that law and politics did not mix and warned him to stay away from "troublemakers" such as Gaur Radebe and Walter Sisulu.

After taking correspondence courses at the University of South Africa, Mandela received his bachelor's degree in 1942. Soon after, he enrolled in law school at the University of Witwatersrand. He continued to work for the law firm as a clerk. Meanwhile, Gaur Radebe and Walter Sisulu continued to educate him with their thoughts on racial equality.

Mandela had brief contact with the Communist Party, a group that believed that all factories, land, and property should be owned in common by everyone in a nation. But Mandela never became a member of the party. He worried that a political organization dominated by whites would not be sensitive

[1] pay through the
     nose 付出过
     高的代价

[2] crumbs （食
     品，尤指面包、
     糕饼的）碎屑

们说。"现在，你们再让我们倾家荡产赎回几块
最贫瘠的土地。"

曼德拉突然明白这些话是多么正确。在整
个地产买卖过程中，法律事务所只有很少的实际
工作要做，却按照常规拿走绝大部分的利润，而
黑人代理人只能分到些残羹冷炙。他工作的事务
所与西苏卢的地产公司合作时，总是狮子大开口
般地拿走最多的地产买卖佣金。

有一次，完成了几件差事后，曼德拉来到希
德尔斯基的办公室。拉德贝也在那里。他若有所
思地打量了一下这位年轻的同事，然后转身朝向
坐在桌子后面的希德尔斯基。"看看，你就像个
君主一样坐在桌子后面，与此同时，我的酋长
（曼德拉）跑来跑去为你效命，"他说。"这种情
况应该颠倒过来，总有一天会的，而且我们还要
把你们统统扔到海里去。"

对于这么冒失的言论，曼德拉十分震惊，可
是希德尔斯基只是摇摇头，并没有说什么。事后
他对曼德拉说，法律与政治不应该彼此混淆，还
警告他与高尔·拉德贝、瓦尔特·西苏卢之类的
"惹是生非者"保持距离。

在南非大学读完函授课程后，曼德拉于
1942年取得了学士学位。之后不久，曼德拉进入
了金山大学法学院，他还继续在事务所里做职
员。同时，高尔·拉德贝和瓦尔特·西苏卢也继
续向他灌输种族平等的思想。

曼德拉与共产党有过短暂的接触，这个团
体认为，一个国家所有的工厂、土地和财产都
应该为全体国民所共有。不过，曼德拉最终没
有加入共产党。他担心一个由白人领导的政治

纳尔逊·曼德拉

to the concerns of black people. Still, he was interested in finding a way to express his feelings about the political injustices in South Africa.

Into the ANC

It was through his friendship with Walter Sisulu that Mandela finally joined the African National Congress. But Mandela did not simply become a member. He became a force within the thirty-year-old organization.

At the time, there was an international groundswell[1] to throw off the yoke[2] of colonialism—the ruling of one nation by another, far-off nation. India was in a state of turmoil[3] as its people pushed for the end of British rule. Similar sparks were flying in the French colonies of Southeast Asia. Africans were starting to demand and win their freedom from European powers, too.

Anton Lembede, one of Africa's leading scholars, wrote about self-rule in an African newspaper. He explained how powerful nations spent huge sums of money to keep their colonies from breaking free. He also explained how some native people were used as pawns[4] by the ruling class. Native people who became educated professionals, Lembede said, often accepted and supported the laws of foreign rulers, instead of fighting against them.

This article caused Mandela to rethink his education and his place in the struggle for freedom. He resolved not to be used as a pawn by white authorities. Instead, he and others began to commit themselves to the ANC. In 1944, Mandela, Anton Lembede, Walter Sisulu, Oliver Tambo, and others formed the Youth League of the ANC. Their goal was the establishment of real

组织不会对黑人的利益给予足够的关心。他还是想要找到一条途径来表达自己对南非政治不公平现状的看法。

加入非国大

因为和瓦尔特·西苏卢的友谊，曼德拉最终加入非洲人国民大会。但曼德拉不仅仅成为该组织的一名成员。他成为这个具有30年历史的组织中一个举足轻重的人物。

当时，在世界范围内，要求结束殖民主义的呼声日益高涨。殖民主义指一个国家被另一个遥远的国家统治。印度国内局势动荡，人民试图推翻英国统治。类似的运动也发生在东南亚的法国殖民地。非洲人民也开始同欧洲列强进行斗争，以求获得自由。

安东·伦贝迪是非洲主要的学者之一，他在一家非洲报纸上就自治的问题发表文章。他阐明了强权国家如何耗费巨资阻止它们的殖民地获得独立。他还解释了一些本土人如何沦为统治阶级的爪牙。伦贝迪说，那些受过教育的本土专业人士往往不是去抗争，而是接受并且支持外国统治者制定的法律。

这篇文章使曼德拉重新审视自己所接受的教育以及自己在争取自由的斗争中所处的位置。他决心不沦为被白人统治者利用的爪牙，而是开始和其他人一起致力于非国大的事业。1944年，曼德拉、安东·伦贝迪、瓦尔特·西苏卢、奥利弗·坦博和其他志士一起组建了非国大青年联盟。他们的目标就是在南非建立起真正的民

[1] groundswell （舆论、群情等）迅速高涨

[2] yoke 枷锁；束缚

[3] turmoil 骚动，动乱

[4] pawns 爪牙，工具

纳尔逊·曼德拉

democracy in South Africa. They would work for political representation for South Africans of all races, the fair distribution of land, good education for all, the removal of restrictions on black trade unions, and the end of discriminatory laws.

Lembede was elected president of the Youth League, while Tambo became secretary and Sisulu treasurer. Mandela served on the Executive Committee. The ANC had always tried to work with the white authorities, but the Youth League pushed instead for black independence and self-rule. The league discouraged white participation, arguing that white members would undermine African self-reliance.

During the league's formative stages, members spent a lot of time planning and working out the details of their organization. Meetings took place in the home of Walter Sisulu. He and his wife, Albertina, were like the parents many of the young men had left behind. There was plenty of food at the house and always a bed for those in need.

Mandela spent a lot of time at the Sisulu home, engaging in discussions or just enjoying the company. But politics wasn't the only pastime at the house. For Mandela, love blossomed there, too. In 1944, he met a girl from rural Transkei. Evelyn Mase was a shy, pretty girl who seemed a bit overwhelmed by the fast pace of the Sisulu household. She was training to be a nurse and lived in nearby Orlando with her brother.

Nelson was touched by Evelyn's quiet beauty, and he began dating her. Their romance progressed quickly. Within a year, they were married in a civil ceremony. It was a far different ceremony than Nelson would have had in the royal kraal. The pomp[1] and prestige of his early life were little more than memories now, but he did not regret the choices he had made. He was happy with his

NELSON MANDELA

主。他们要成为南非所有种族人民的政治代表，争取土地的公平分配，让所有人受到良好的教育，终止对黑人商业联盟的限制，废除歧视性法律。

伦贝迪当选为青年联盟主席，坦博为书记，西苏卢为财务总管。曼德拉负责执行委员会的工作。非国大一直试图与白人当权者展开合作，但是青年联盟则奋力争取黑人独立与自治。联盟拒绝白人的参与，认为白人成员会削弱非洲人的自主性。

在青年联盟的创始阶段，各成员花去大量时间计划和制定组织的各个细节。会议在瓦尔特·西苏卢家里进行。他和妻子阿尔贝蒂娜就像是许多与会年轻人的父母。房子里永远有充足的食物，谁要是困了，就可以得到一张床铺。

曼德拉在西苏卢家里度过了许多时光，有时是参加讨论，有时纯粹是朋友间的交往。但政治并非是这里唯一的活动。对于曼德拉来说，爱情之花也在这里盛开了。1944年，他遇到了一个来自特兰斯凯乡村的女孩。伊夫琳·梅思是个羞涩、漂亮的姑娘，她对于西苏卢家的快节奏有点无所适从。她当时正在学习护士课程，和她的兄弟一道住在附近的奥兰多。

纳尔逊被姑娘安静的美所打动，并开始和她约会。他们的恋爱进展很快。不到一年，他们就举行了世俗婚礼。这场婚礼与纳尔逊在王室村庄可能享受到的婚礼大相径庭。他早年所享有的荣光与声望如今已成为了回忆，但是他没有为自己的选择而后悔。

[1] pomp 华丽，壮观；盛况

纳尔逊·曼德拉

life despite the hardships.

As a black couple, Nelson and Evelyn faced the challenge of finding a decent house in Johannesburg. That was not easy. Blacks were restricted to certain areas of the city. Eventually, the couple found a small home in West Orlando, part of the township of Soweto. There they started a family. Their first child, born in 1946, was a boy named Madiba Thembelike Mandela. Within a decade, the couple would have two more children: a son named Makgatho and a daughter, Mkakaziwe, who died when she was just nine months old. All the while, Mandela not only continued his work with the ANC, he intensified[1] it.

虽然生活很艰辛，但是他依然快乐。

　　作为一对黑人夫妇，要在约翰内斯堡找到一处体面的房子对于纳尔逊和伊夫琳来说是一项挑战。那不容易。黑人被限制在城市中几个特定的区域里。最终，夫妇俩在位于索韦托黑人居住区的西奥兰多找到了一间小房子。他们在那里开始了家庭生活。他们的第一个孩子出生于1946年，是个男孩，名叫马迪巴·坦贝莱克·曼德拉。在接下去的10年里，夫妇俩又有了两个孩子：男孩马加托和女孩姆卡卡吉维，女孩在9个月大的时候夭折了。在这期间，曼德拉不仅继续为非国大工作，并且使这个组织不断壮大起来。

[1] intensified　加
强

纳
尔
逊
·
曼
德
拉

CHAPTER SIX

A REVOLUTIONARY SPIRIT

革 命 精 神

World War II in Europe ended in 1945 with the destruction of Hitler's Nazi army. Black South Africans had participated in the war effort. They were proud to help bring an end to the racism of the Nazi regime. Next they wanted to see racism stamped out in their own country. ANC leaders, particularly in the Youth League, were optimistic. Now they could achieve their own goals, or so they thought. As it turned out, they were wrong. Two events taught them something they would not forget.

By this time South Africa was an independent nation enjoying a peaceful relationship with England. Yet whites still governed South Africa and imposed oppressive policies on others. In 1946, Prime Minister Jan Smut passed the Asiatic Land Tenure Act. It was nicknamed "the Ghetto Act" because it restricted the movement of East Indian people in South Africa and limited them to certain ghettos, or neighborhoods. The action was a sharp reminder that discrimination was still alive and was not restricted to the blacks of the country.

The Indian community responded with a wave of protests. They continued their campaign for two years, and many of the movement's leaders landed in jail. The ANC leadership was greatly impressed by

this effort. Inspired by the Indian leaders, the ANC heads no longer feared going to prison in the struggle for black civil rights.

Another event that year—a mine workers strike—added to their sense of resolve. Mining was one of South Africa's largest industries and was responsible for much of the nation's wealth. But mining also exploited the Africans who worked in the mines. Mining

　　1945年，在欧洲战场，第二次世界大战以希特勒的纳粹军队被击败而结束。南非的黑人也参与了战争。他们为打败纳粹政权的种族主义做出了贡献，并为此感到自豪。接下来，他们想看到自己国家中的种族主义被消灭。非国大的领袖们，尤其是青年联盟的领袖们十分乐观。现在正是他们实现目标的时机，或者说他们是这样想的。但事实证明，他们错了。两个事件教会了他们一些无法忘记的东西。

　　到这个时候，南非是个独立的国家，与英国保持着和平的关系。但白人统治着南非，对其他种族施以压迫性的政策。1946年，首相简·斯马特签署了《亚洲人土地使用法》。该法案绰号为"聚居区法"，原因是它限制了东印度人在南非的活动自由，将他们限制在某些聚居区或街区之内。该法案表明，歧视仍然存在，而且针对的不仅仅是这个国家内的黑人。

　　作为回应，印度民众进行了多次抗议。这样的运动持续了两年，许多运动领袖被捕入狱。这一系列运动给非国大领导层带来极大触动。非国大首脑们受到印度领袖们的鼓舞，入狱的威胁已无法阻挡他们为黑人权利而斗争。

　　那一年发生的另一件事——矿工罢工——更加坚定了他们的信念。采矿业是南非支柱产业之一，创造了大量的国家财富。但采矿业是对非洲工人的剥削，采矿的工作

was dangerous, health-threatening work, for which blacks were paid a fraction[1] of the wages of their white counterparts. Discontentment[2] among the workers had been brewing[3] for years, but in 1946 it came to a head.

Calling for a wage of ten shillings a day, a two-week paid vacation a year, and decent housing for workers and their families, 70,000 miners went on strike. The strike was led by J. B. Marks, president of the mine workers union; Gaur Radebe; and Moses Kotane. All were members of the ANC and the Communist Party.

Though the strike was nonviolent, it was illegal, and the government sent a small army of police with rifles, bayonets[4], and batons[5] against the strikers. Within a week, at least nine miners had been killed and 1,248 others had been injured. The strike was brutally crushed, and Marks, Kotane, and fifty-two others were jailed. It was a sign of things to come.

The Nationalists

Soon things went from bad to worse for black South Africans. By law, non-whites—eighty percent of the country's population—were barred[6] from voting in elections. In 1948, the country's white voters put the Nationalist Party into office. It took up the reigns of power under the leadership of Prime Minister Daniel Malan.

Malan and many other Nationalists were Afrikaners who were hostile

to the English. Some Nationalists had even supported Germany during World War II. The Nationalists were particularly hateful toward blacks. They warned about what they called the *swart gevaar*, or "black threat." During the campaign, the Nationalists had repeatedly shouted, "*Die kaffer op sy plek*" (the nigger in his place) and "*Die koelies uit die land*" (the coolies[7] out of the country). The word coolie

NELSON MANDELA

很危险，对健康危害也很大，而黑人矿工的工资只是他们白人同事的一小部分。不满情绪在工人中已经存在了许多年，在1946年这种愤怒到达了顶点。

为了获得10先令的日薪和每年两周的带薪假期，以及让工人和他们的家庭拥有像样的住房，7万名矿工举行罢工。罢工由矿工联合会主席马克斯、高尔·拉德贝以及摩西·孔塔尼领导，他们既是非国大成员也是共产党员。

虽然工人采取非暴力的形式进行罢工，但仍是违法的，政府派出一支装备有来复枪、刺刀、警棍的小型武装警察部队对抗罢工者。不到一周的时间里，至少有9名矿工被杀，另外还有1 248人受伤。罢工被残酷地镇压了，马克斯、孔塔尼以及另外52人被捕入狱。这一事件成为后来一系列事件的前兆。

国民党

很快，对于南非的黑人来说，事情变得更加糟糕了。根据法律，占该国人口8成的非白色人种在选举中没有选举权。1948年，该国白人选民将国民党选上了台。以丹尼尔·马兰为首相的政党开始操控权力。

马兰和许多国民党人是南非白人，对英国持有敌对态度。一些国民党党员甚至在第二次世界大战期间帮助过德国。国民党尤其痛恨黑人。他们宣扬他们所谓的"黑人威胁论"。竞选期间，国民党就一再叫嚣"黑鬼滚回老家去"以及"苦力从这个国家滚出去"。"苦力"一词

[1] fraction 小部分
[2] Discontentment 不满
[3] brewing （尤指不利的事、坏事）酝酿着；发展中
[4] bayonets （步枪上的）刺刀
[5] batons 警棍
[6] barred 禁止
[7] coolies 苦力，苦工（尤指旧时印度、中国及亚洲其他国家的非技术工人）

纳尔逊·曼德拉

was an insulting term for anyone from Asia, including those from India.

Nationalist Party ideas could be grouped under one word, *apartheid* [1]. It was a word few in the outside world had heard before. Apartheid means "apartness"—separation of the races. Some people claimed apartheid would help preserve the many cultures in South Africa, including the small tribal groups. Few took that explanation seriously, however. Most observers saw apartheid for what it was: a new word for the old idea of white supremacy.

Malan wasted no time in implementing the system of racial discrimination he championed. In 1950, his government passed two laws that stood at the very heart of apartheid. The first was the Population Registration Act, which labeled everyone in South Africa according to race. The second was the Group Areas Act, which forced different racial groups to live in different places.

In 1951, the government passed two more infamous laws. The Separate Representation of Voters Act transferred mixed-race, or "colored" South Africans to separate voting rolls. Under this system, colored South Africans could vote. But their votes did not carry much weight. Representatives they elected had no direct voice in government. That same year, the government abolished the Native Representation Council, a government advisory panel made up of black representatives.

Attitudes toward blacks, coloreds, and Indians hardened significantly during this period. Apartheid brought restriction in every area of work, schooling, housing, and family life. Nelson Mandela would later describe the system:

An African child is born in an Africans Only hospital, taken home in an Africans Only bus, lives in an Africans Only area, and

是对包括印度在内的来自亚洲的所有人的侮辱性称呼。

国民党的政策可以归结为一个词："种族隔离"。人们在其他国家几乎没有听过这个词，它的意思是"隔离"——将种族分隔开来，有些人宣称这有助于保护南非众多的文化，包括那些小部落的文化在内。然而，几乎没人会真的相信这种论调。大多数观察家都看出了其本来的面目：是对于老套的"白人优势论"的新的表达方式。

马兰急不可耐地实施其主张的种族歧视制度。1950年，他的政府通过了两部在种族隔离制度中占核心地位的法律。第一部是《人口登记法》，它将每个南非人按种族进行分类。第二部是《种族区域法》，强行规定不同的种族群体必须居住在不同的区域内。

1951年，该政府还通过了另两部声名狼藉的法律《代表分离法案》将混血人种或南非"有色"人种转移至单独的投票名单上。在这一制度下，南非的有色人种有选举权，但是他们的选票没有什么分量。他们选出的代表在政府中没有直接发言权。同年，政府解散了黑人代表委员会——一个由黑人代表组成的政府顾问小组。

在这一时期，针对黑人、有色人种以及印度人的态度强硬了许多。种族隔离给工作、教育、住房以及家庭生活的每一方面都带来了诸多限制。纳尔逊·曼德拉后来对这一政策是这样描述的：

一个非洲小孩在一家仅限非洲人的医院出生，坐仅限非洲人的公车回家，住在仅限非洲人的地区，

[1] apartheid（尤指南非当局对黑人及其他有色人种实行的）种族隔离（制）

纳尔逊·曼德拉

attends Africans Only schools, if he attends school at all.

When he grows up, he can hold Africans Only jobs, rent a house in Africans Only townships, ride Africans Only trains and be stopped any time of the day or night and be ordered to produce a pass, failing which he will be arrested and thrown in jail. His life is circumscribed[1] *by racist laws and regulations that cripple his growth, dim his potential, and stunt his life.*

By 1952, the Nationalist government was well on its way to cementing[2] its dream of a segregated[3] society in which Afrikaners dominated all other ethnic groups. Party members were filled with near-religious fervor[4]. It had been 300 years since the Boer founding father, Jan van Riebeeck, had established a colony in the region. The Afrikaners took their ability to survive for three centuries as a sign that they were God's chosen people. They set about securing their victory by outlawing nearly every legal form of protest.

Mayibuye Afrika: Let Africa Return

By 1952 Nelson Mandela was president of the ANC Youth League, and he wanted a change in tactics. As Afrikaners celebrated their tricentennial[5], the ANC drafted a letter to Prime Minister Malan. In it, they explained that they had exhausted all constitutional means of achiev-

ing rights for the black population. They demanded a repeal[6] of the unjust laws that formed the basis of apartheid. If no action was taken, the organization would have to resort to extra-constitutional measures.

Malan's reply made it clear that his government had no intention of meeting the ANC's demands. The prime minister stressed his desire to preserve white rule in South

进入仅限非洲人的学校，如果他上学的话。

他长大以后，从事仅限非洲人的工作，在仅限非洲人的居住区租一套房子，坐仅限非洲人的火车，不分昼夜，随时随地被叫住查验通行证，要是没有通行证，就会被抓起来投入大牢。他的一生由种族主义法律和规定所限定，成长被破坏，天赋被埋没，生命被压抑。

到了1952年，国民党政府正一步步实现他们的野心，建立一个由南非白人统治所有其他种族的种族隔离的社会。该党成员充满了近乎宗教的狂热，那时距离布尔的开国者简·范·里贝克在这一地区建立起殖民地已经有300年的时间了。南非白人将自己视作神挑选出来的子民，因为他们在这里已经生存了3个世纪。为了保护自己的胜利成果，他们将几乎一切合法的抗议形式宣布为非法。

回来，非洲：让非洲回归

到1952年，纳尔逊·曼德拉成为非国大青年联盟的主席，他希望对策略进行调整。当南非白人庆祝他们的300周年纪念日时，非国大起草了一封给首相马兰的信。信中阐明，为了争取黑人的权利，他们已经用尽全部宪法允许的方法，他们要求废除构成种族隔离的不平等法律，如果政府不采取行动，组织将不得不动用超出宪法范围的手段。

纳尔逊·曼德拉得到的回答很明确，政府无意满足非国大的要求，首相强调了他保持白人在南非统治地位的决心，并发

[1] circumscribed
限定；划分出

[2] cementing 巩固，加强；使正式确定

[3] segregated
种族隔离的

[4] fervor 热情；热烈

[5] tricentennial
300周年纪念日

[6] repeal （法令等的）废除

Africa and promised to use force if necessary to quell[1] any black unrest. "We regarded Malan's curt[2] dismissal of our demands as a declaration of war," Mandela wrote in his autobiography. "We had no alternative but to resort to civil disobedience[3], and we embarked on preparations for mass action in earnest[4]." That was the start of the Defiance Campaign.

On June 26, 1952, ANC leadership called for a national strike. Blacks, Indians, and coloreds marched through areas marked "Whites Only" and refused to carry passbooks that designated their racial status. Malan was as good as his word and met the strikers with mass arrests and police brutality. Mandela, Sisulu, and others were arrested.

But the strikers continued their efforts throughout the remainder of the year. The oppressed people of the country had awakened and did not plan another slumber[5]. Walter Sisulu seemed to speak for many involved in the campaign when he made a statement upon his arrest.

"As long as I enjoy the confidence of my people, and as long as there is a spark of life and energy in me, I shall fight with courage and determination for the abolition of discriminatory laws and for the freedom of all South Africans," he said. He spent a week in jail rather than pay the fines that would have gotten him out immediately.

The Defiance Campaign was largely nonviolent. In fact, international observers commented repeatedly on the peaceful nature of the protests. Yet confrontations sometimes did turn violent, often in response to police brutality. In New Brighton in October 1952, for instance, a white policeman shot two blacks who were suspected of theft. A crowd reacted angrily, and the policeman pumped more than twenty bullets into the charging mass before escaping. People continued their rampage[6], and before peace returned, seven

[1] quell 镇压（叛乱等）；平息

[2] curt 草率无礼的；生硬的

[3] disobedience 不服从，违抗

[4] in earnest 认真地；诚挚地

[5] slumber 睡眠

[6] rampage 暴跳；横冲直撞

誓如有必要就会动用武力镇压任何黑人的骚乱。"马兰草率打发了我们的要求，我们将其视为宣战，"纳尔逊·曼德拉在自传中写道。"我们别无选择，只能发动公民不服从运动，并且我们开始认真准备大规模行动。"那便是蔑视运动的开端。

在1952年6月26日，非国大领导层号召全国开展大罢工，黑人、印度人以及其他有色人种游行示威，进入那些标明"仅限白人"的地区，拒绝携带标有种族身份的通行证。像马兰放出的话那样，他动用警察进行残酷镇压，大规模逮捕游行者。曼德拉、西苏卢和其他一些人一同被捕。

然而，罢工一直持续到当年年底。整个国家里受压迫的人民觉醒了，这一回他们不会再睡去。当瓦尔特·西苏卢被捕时，他发表了一个声明，他的声音似乎代表了许多参加运动的人。

"只要我尚能感受到我的人民的信心，只要我仍有一点生命的能量，我就将满怀勇气与决心，为铲除歧视性的法律，为所有南非人民的自由而战斗不息，"他说。他宁愿在监狱中度过一周的时间也不愿意为立即获释而缴纳罚款。

蔑视运动在很大程度上属于非暴力运动。事实上，国际观察家曾多次指出这一系列抗议活动的非暴力性。不过，对抗有时的确会转变成暴力，这种情况通常是由于警察的残酷镇压。比如，1952年10月，在纽布莱顿，一名白人警察因怀疑两名黑人偷窃而将他们射杀。人群愤怒了，该警察朝冲过来的人群连开二十几枪，随后逃离。群众愈加愤怒，等最终事态平息时，

blacks and four whites were dead. Another twenty-seven people were injured. The government used this example of unrest as an excuse to clamp down[1] even harder on the Defiance Campaign.

In addition to arresting thousands of protesters, the government "banned" more than fifty strike leaders. Under South African law, a banned person was restricted from traveling, making public appearances, speaking with other banned individuals, and participating in many other activities. By December 1952, arrests, bannings, and other government actions had halted the Defiance Campaign.

Mandela, Sisulu, and others were placed on trial as Communists. However, the courts refused to convict the men on the most serious charges of antigovernment activity. They were given nine-month suspended sentences, which amounted to little more than slaps on the wrist.

The movement had gained ground[2]. The ANC had succeeded in creating a united front against apartheid. It had focused world attention on the injustices in South Africa and had sprung into prominence. Membership increased greatly.

Yet, while Mandela and the other leaders celebrated these successes, the government in the capital city of Pretoria launched a defiance campaign of its own. Without a trial or formal charges, the government issued expanded banning orders against the bulk[3] of the ANC leadership. It also declared that protesters could be whipped, jailed for up to three years, fined the equivalent[4] of nearly $1,000, or be given any two of these penalties combined. Encouraging protest was punishable by an additional two years in prison or the equivalent of $500 in fines. These rulings forced

NELSON MANDELA

已经有7名黑人和4名白人死于非命了。此外还有27人受伤。政府以此次骚乱为借口，对蔑视运动施以更加残酷的镇压。

政府不仅抓捕了数以千计的抗议者，还对超过50名的罢工领袖施以"禁令"。根据当时的南非法律，被施以禁令的人被禁止外出旅行，被禁止在公共场所出现，被禁止与其他有禁令在身的人交谈，被禁止参加许多其他的活动。到了1952年12月，逮捕、禁令以及其他政府行为已经将蔑视运动打压下去了。

曼德拉、西苏卢和其他人以共产党的身份被审判。然而，对于这些被指控犯有最严重的反政府罪行的人，法庭拒绝判他们有罪。最后，他们被判了9个月的缓刑，这样的惩罚就像打几下手腕。

运动已经取得了进展。非国大已经建立了反对种族隔离的联合前线。它已经把世界的目光集中到南非的不公平现状上，并且已经成为一个优秀的组织。组织的成员增加了许多。

然而，正当曼德拉和其他领导人庆祝胜利的时候，政府在首都城市比勒陀利亚也发动了一场蔑视运动。未经审讯或任何正式的指控，政府就宣布了对大批非国大领导人的禁令。它还宣布抗议者将会被鞭答，被判长达3年的徒刑，被处以相当于$1 000的罚款，或是这其中任何二者合一的惩罚。鼓动抗议者另加2年监禁或是相当于$500的罚款。这些规定让非国大不得不重

[1] clamp down
采取行动禁止（或制止）

[2] gained ground
前进，发展

[3] bulk 大部分

[4] equivalent 相等物

纳尔逊·曼德拉

the ANC to reconsider its strategy.

Practicing Law

Mandela managed to complete his law degree, despite the Defiance Campaign and his other work with the ANC. He had quit his job at Witkin, Sidelsky and Eidelman and had gained experience working for several other white law firms. He was shocked by the fact that even the most reputable firms charged black clients far more than whites. There were no black law firms in the area, so Mandela decided to start one.

In August 1952, he went out on his own. Within a short time, he asked his old schoolmate Oliver Tambo to join him in the practice. Tambo was a brilliant law student and was committed to civil rights. The partners opened a practice in downtown Johannesburg. Black clients flocked to the office. Every morning, the two lawyers had to wade[1] through long lines of waiting clients just to open their doors. Mandela later explained why black South Africans needed so much assistance:

Africans were desperate for legal help...it was a crime to walk through a Whites Only door, a crime to ride a Whites Only bus, a crime to use a Whites Only drinking fountain, a crime to walk on a Whites Only beach, a crime to be on the streets after eleven, a crime not to have a pass book and a crime to have the wrong signature in that book, a crime to be unemployed and a crime to be employed in the wrong place, a crime to live in certain places and a crime to have no place to live.

NELSON MANDELA

Mandela and Tambo quickly discovered that the practice of the law on behalf of blacks in South Africa was an act of defiance in itself.

The partners turned out to be an excellent match. Tambo, a quiet and patient man, was the workhorse of the firm. Mandela, with

新考虑其战略。

做律师

曼德拉在参与蔑视运动和完成非国大其他工作的同时也获得了法律学位。他已经不再为威特金、希德尔斯基和埃德尔曼律师事务所工作了，通过为其他几家白人律师事务所工作，他积累了经验。他震惊于这样的事实，即便声誉最好的事务所，给黑人主顾开出的价码也要远远高于白人。曼德拉所在的地区还没有黑人律师事务所，于是他决定要开创先河。

在1952年8月，他一个人开始行动了。没多久，他邀请老同学奥利弗·坦博加入他的律师工作。坦博是法学优等生，致力于公民权利事业。这对搭档在约翰内斯堡市区开业。黑人顾客蜂拥而至。每天早晨，两位律师总要费力地通过长长的在等候的人群队伍才能把办公室的门打开。曼德拉后来解释为什么南非黑人需要这么多的帮助：

非洲人极度渴望法律援助……走进仅限白人的门是犯罪，搭乘仅限白人的公共汽车是犯罪，使用仅限白人的喷泉式饮水器是犯罪，在仅限白人的沙滩上行走是犯罪，11点钟后出现在街上是犯罪，没有通行证是犯罪，通行证上的签名错误也是犯罪，失业是犯罪，在错误的地方就业也是犯罪，在某些区域居住是犯罪，无处居住也是犯罪。

曼德拉和坦博很快发觉，在南非代表黑人开展法律业务，其本身就是一种蔑视行为。

两位搭档间的配合十分出色。坦博安静而有耐心，他是事务所里吃苦耐劳的人。曼德拉说话

[1] wade （通过水、雪、泥沙等妨碍物）艰难地行进

a more flamboyant[1] speaking style, was the perfect trial attorney. Together, they earned respect from the courts and other attorneys. Had they lived in a less oppressive country, they may have led simple lives of quiet comfort. But that was not to be.

Eventually, the partners were forced to move their offices, since they were set up in an area designated for whites only. It was harder for clients to reach the new offices on the outskirts of the city, and the move hurt the business considerably.

Burdens of the Struggle

By 1953, the Mandela marriage had gotten rocky. Nelson loved his family and was a dedicated father, but his schedule often took him away from home. Even when he was in town, he worked long hours and increasingly became a stranger to his family.

About the same time, Evelyn became a Jehovah's Witness[2]. She embraced her new religion with a passion that matched Nelson's zeal[3] for politics. But the change created a rift[4] between the couple that grew day by day. Evelyn felt that her husband should put his faith in God and worry less about the fight for equality. He believed that a religious life had merit, but he wasn't willing to give up politics for it.

Nelson and Evelyn found themselves on entirely different paths and divorced in 1955. Nelson maintained a strong relationship with his children, and he missed the life of a married man. But he could grieve the loss of his marriage for only so long. The movement called, and he continued to answer it.

The government in Pretoria continued to reshape South African society according to the ideals of the Nationalist Party. In 1953,

[1] flamboyant 浮夸的

口若悬河，是一位卓越的审讯律师。在这样的合作下，他们赢得了法庭以及其他代理律师的尊重。如果是在一个少有压迫的国度里，他们也许就此过上平静舒适的生活。然而那是不可能的。

最终，两个搭档被迫将办公室迁往别处，因为它们是在标明仅限白人的地区。新办公室位于郊区，委托人去那里更不方便了，这次搬迁严重打击了事务所的业务。

斗争的负担

到了1953年，曼德拉的婚姻已变得摇摇欲坠。纳尔逊爱他的家，是个尽责的父亲，可是他的日程安排使他没有在家的时间。就算在镇上，他也要工作很长的时间，这使他与自己的家庭越来越疏远。

[2] Jehovah's Witness 耶和华见证人（约于1879年在美国成立的一基督教组织，认为世界末日在即，只有"耶和华见证人"才能逃过劫难）

[3] zeal 热情
[4] rift 裂痕

与此同时，伊夫琳成为一位"耶和华见证人"。她对新的宗教信仰的激情与纳尔逊对政治的热情简直是旗鼓相当。然而这种变化使夫妻间产生了裂痕，并随着时间的流逝而越来越严重。伊夫琳觉得丈夫应该将信仰归于上帝，少一些为平等而抗争所带来的忧虑。他认为宗教生活虽然有益，但他不会因此而放弃政治。

纳尔逊和伊夫琳发现他们已经走上了截然不同的道路，最终于1955年离婚。纳尔逊与他的孩子们仍保持着亲密的关系，他对于婚姻生活也十分怀念。但是他没有多少伤感的时间。运动的召唤使他必须继续向前。

比勒陀利亚政府继续按照国民党的理想对南非社会进行改造。在1953年，《班图（黑

it passed the Bantu [black] Education Act, which ended funding for the religious schools that had educated blacks like Mandela. The law was obviously designed to keep the black population as ignorant as possible. The minister of Bantu Education, Dr. Hendrik Verwoerd, made that clear in a statement published shortly after the law was passed: "[Education] must train and teach people in accordance with their opportunities in life....There is no place for the [black] in the European community above the level of certain forms of labor."

That year, a number of black communities responded to the law by boycotting government-run schools and setting up alternative schools[1] called "culture clubs." These schools were independent and couldn't be controlled by the government. Soon Verwoerd declared that the alternative schools were illegal.

Black leaders were outraged[2] and renewed their struggle. Under the new leadership of Albert Luthuli, the ANC organized a People's Congress. It drew delegates from all over the country and from all different ethnic groups. Even some sympathetic whites were a part of the first meeting, which took place in June 1955 in the small multiracial village of Kliptown, a few miles southwest of Johannesburg.

More than 3,000 people took part. They arrived by car, bus, truck, and even on foot. There was also a small army of police around, snapping pictures and recording the events in small notebooks.

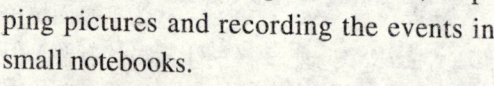

The gathering was a fantastic sight. Songs were sung in Zulu, Xhosa, and English. There were dozens of impassioned speeches designed to create a sense of unity. But the real work of the two-day conference was the drafting of the Freedom Charter. It called for a radically different South Africa

人）教育法》中止了对宗教学校的拨款，这些学校的学生正是像曼德拉这样的黑人。很明显，该法案企图对黑人实行愚民政策。班图教育大臣亨德里克·维尔沃尔德博士在法案得到通过后不久的一份声明中清楚地表达了这一目的："（教育）必须培养和教会人们安于生活的现状……在欧洲社会，高于劳工的任何阶层中都没有（黑人）的容身之地。"

那一年，作为对该法案的回应，数个黑人社区联合抵制政府公办的学校，并创立了非传统学校，称为"文化俱乐部"。这些学校是独立的，不受政府控制。很快，维尔沃尔德就宣布这些非传统学校非法。

黑人领袖们被激怒了，并再次开始反抗。在新领袖艾伯特·卢图利的带领下，非国大组织了人民大会。大会代表从全国各地以及各个种族中选出。甚至一些同情黑人的白人也参加了第一次大会，这次会议于1955年6月在多种族聚居的克力普顿小村庄举行，该村庄位于约翰内斯堡西南几英里处。

有3 000多人参加了会议。他们乘坐小汽车、公共汽车和卡车来到会场，有的甚至步行前来。会场周围有一支小型武装警察部队，他们不停地拍照，还在小本子上记录着现场的各种情况。

集会场面十分壮观。人们用祖鲁语、科萨语以及英语唱歌。许多激动人心的演讲力图创造出团结的氛围。不过为期两天的会议的主要任务是起草《自由宪章》。这部宪章要求建立一个与以往有很大不同的南非，在这

[1] alternative schools 非传统学校（指因对现存教育制度不满而在组织、目标、教学方法方面采取非传统措施的中、小学）

[2] outraged 使震惊；使愤慨

纳尔逊·曼德拉

in which: "The People Shall Govern. All National Groups Shall Have Equal Rights. The People Shall Share In The Country's Wealth. The Land Shall Be Shared Among Those Who Work It...."

The charter was a revolutionary document and most delegates were pleased with it, but they never got to vote on it. On the second day of the conference, police charged the speaker's platform, pushing delegates off the stage and accusing them of treason[1].

The authorities successfully broke up the conference, but they did not stop the world from taking notice and declaring the conference one of the most remarkable political gatherings of modern times.

Within three months, the government responded to the People's Congress. Invoking[2] the Suppression of Communism Act, the police arrested anyone suspected of opposing government policies. In December 1956, Mandela was arrested again. He, along with 155 others, was to be placed on trial for high treason.

While the arrests were meant to silence dissent[3], they accomplished just the opposite. Because of banning orders, people who had been unable to talk with one another outside of prison now found themselves together in large cells. Old friends and comrades became reacquainted, while younger activists listened and learned. Instead of the sad desperation that often overtakes those in jail, there was an air of celebration.

The people began to realize a power that the government could not contain with its guns and batons.

Not long after the arrests, the prisoners were released. But they were under strict banning orders until their trials. They could not travel or speak in public. Mandela was a primary target of such orders, as were others in high command of the ANC.

样一个国家里："国家由人民管理。所有的民族都拥有平等的权利。人民有权共享国家的财富。土地应由在它上面劳作的人共享……"

该宪章是一部革命性的文件，并且得到了大多数代表的认可，然而他们没来得及对文件进行投票表决。大会进行的第二天，警察冲向演讲台，将代表们推下台，还指控他们犯有叛国罪。

当局摧毁了大会，然而他们无法阻止全世界关注的目光，大会已经被公认为现代最具影响力的政治集会之一。

不到3个月，政府对人民大会作出了回应。根据《镇压共产主义法令》，警察逮捕了任何被怀疑反对政府政策的人。1956年12月，曼德拉再次被捕，他与其他155人将以严重叛国罪接受审判。

抓捕是为了消除异议，可是事情恰恰相反。本来由于禁令在监狱外无法彼此交流的人，现在发现他们在大牢里相聚了，老朋友还有老同志彼此之间又变得熟悉起来，而较年轻的激进主义分子在聆听和学习。与一般弥漫在监狱中的绝望哀伤不同，这里有一种欢庆的气氛。人们开始意识到一种政府用枪和棍棒无法限制的力量。

被捕没多久，犯人就被释放了，但是他们受到禁令的严格限制，不能外出旅行，不能在公共场所发表言论。曼德拉是这些禁令的主要目标，非国大其他高层领导人也一样。

[1] treason　叛国罪

[2] Invoking　行使；诉诸（尤指法律和权利）

[3] dissent　异议

纳尔逊·曼德拉

Even with the banning orders, the ANC leadership called for a stay-at-home action in June of 1957. As a form of protest, black people were instructed not to go to work. The action was a remarkable success. In some places, sixty to eighty percent of the black workforce stayed off the job for several days.

Revolutionary Love

In the fall of 1957, Mandela put his time and energy into the upcoming treason trials. If the men were found guilty, they faced lengthy prison terms and a substantial blow to the movement. Those thoughts weighed heavily on Mandela's mind as he negotiated[1] the traffic of downtown Johannesburg one day.

As he passed the finest black hospital in the city, there, standing at the bus stop, was a beautiful young woman. He could not help craning his neck to get a better look at her. Mandela was surprised by his interest in the woman. His marriage had fallen apart largely because of his involvement in the ANC. Without actually admitting it, he had resigned himself to the lonely life of a freedom fighter. If he did have a marriage, it was to the struggle.

Still, the woman on the corner made him feel like a boy of sixteen. Her eyes, her face, her bearing made him want to stop and talk. But there were other matters that required his attention. He scolded himself for thinking he had the luxury of romance at this point and drove on by.

Over the next few weeks, he found himself thinking about the woman at the bus stop. Somehow, her face had etched[2] itself in his memory. That was why he was so amazed one day when he saw the woman seated in

即便有这些禁令，非国大仍于1957年6月发起了一项"不出家门"的活动。作为一种抗议形式，他们号召黑人不要去上班。这次行动取得了卓越的胜利。在一些地区，6到8成的黑人劳动者拒绝上班达数天之久。

革命的爱情

1957年的秋天，曼德拉将时间与精力投入到即将到来的叛国罪审判中。如果这些人被判有罪，他们将面临漫长的牢狱之灾，整个运动也将受到致命的打击。一天，当曼德拉穿过约翰内斯堡市中心的车流时，这些想法沉重地压在他的心头。

当他路过城中最好的黑人医院时，车站那里站着一位美丽的年轻女子。他不禁伸长脖子想好好看看她。曼德拉为自己对她的兴趣感到吃惊。他婚姻的失败很大程度上是由于他参加了非国大。虽然没有承认，但他已将自己变成了一个孤独的自由战士。如果他真的有婚姻，那就是与斗争的结合。

街角的女子还是让他感觉自己像个16岁的男孩，她的双眸、她的脸蛋、她的举止，让他想要停下来和她说话。可是他还有其他重要的事要做。他责骂自己，因为自己在这样的时刻还有浪漫的闲情逸致，他继续开车离开了。

在接下去的几周里，他发现自己一直想着车站的那个女子。不知怎么地，她的容貌已刻进了他的记忆。因此，那天当他看见那个女

[1] negotiated 成功地通过（或越过）（障碍等）

[2] etched 铭记，铭刻

纳尔逊·曼德拉

the office of his partner, Oliver Tambo. She and her brother were there to discuss a legal problem.

Mandela listened to what they had to say, but he had a hard time taking it in. He thought about the woman's eyes, her face, and her lips. About the only thing that stuck in his memory was her name, Nomzamo Winifred Madikizela. It meant "going through trials, one who strives." He knew in an instant the signs of love, and he didn't fight the feeling. Instead, he asked "Winnie" on a date. Had he been a high school student, he could not have been more infatuated[1].

On their first date, Nelson talked about the pending[2] treason case and his life in the struggle. He also told her that he wanted to marry her. It is doubtful that Winnie took this mention of marriage seriously. However, the couple began to see one another regularly. She met his children, watched him work out at the gym, and accompanied him on many activities. To his delight, he quickly discovered that Winnie was as committed to the liberation of black South Africans as he was. Within a year, on June 15, 1958, the couple married.

Winnie's parents were proud to have such a famous and respected man in their family. Still, Winnie's father warned her that she was not just marrying a man. She was marrying the ANC as well. He also warned that she might be criticized for marrying a divorced man. Traditional African society frowned on divorce, particularly for those connected to royalty, as was Mandela.

From the beginning, Winnie and Nelson's lives were dominated by politics. To even get married, Nelson had to apply for a temporary relaxation of the banning orders that restricted his travel. He was allowed to leave Johannesburg for less than a week, to

NELSON MANDELA

子坐在合伙人坦博的办公室里时，他大吃一惊。她和她的兄弟是来进行法律咨询的。

曼德拉虽然在听他们讲话，但很难听进去。他想着那女子的眼睛、她的脸庞，还有她的嘴唇。恐怕他总共只记住一样东西，就是她的姓名——诺姆撒莫·温妮弗莱德·马迪基泽拉，意思是"奋斗的人，渡过难关"。他立刻感觉到了爱情的迹象，他没有压抑这种情感，而是向"温妮"提出了约会的请求。就算是高中生，也不会比他更迷恋对方了。

在他们第一次约会的时候，曼德拉讲了自己悬而未决的叛国罪案件和充满斗争的人生。他还告诉她他想娶她。温妮是否把这求婚当真是值得怀疑的。不过这对情侣开始经常约会。她见了他的几个孩子，看他在体育馆里锻炼，还陪他参加许多活动。让他欣喜的是，他很快发现温妮和他一样献身于南非黑人解放的事业。不到一年，在1958年6月15日，这对情侣结婚了。

温妮的父母为家里多了一位如此著名、如此受人尊重的成员而感到骄傲。尽管如此，温妮的父亲告诫她说，她嫁的不仅仅是一个男人，她还嫁给了非国大。他还告诫她说，她可能受到责难，因为她嫁给了一个离过婚的男人。传统非洲社会对离婚持有偏见，尤其是对那些与王室有关联、类似曼德拉这样的人。

从一开始，温妮和曼德拉的生活就为政治所左右。甚至仅仅是为了结婚，曼德拉就不得不提出申请，请求暂时放松对他不能外出旅行的禁令。他获准可以离开约翰内斯堡不到一周，去

[1] infatuated 迷恋着的

[2] pending 未决的，未定的

travel to the Transkei for the wedding.

On Trial for Treason

The Mandelas did not have much of a honeymoon. The treason trial formally opened the same month they were married. Charges had been dismissed against most of the original 156 protesters. But charges stood against thirty of the most prominent figures, including Mandela, who sat in jail while the trial proceeded.

In the midst of the high-profile trial, unrest continued in the black townships. In a peaceful protest at a train station in 1960, a group of blacks refused to present their passbooks, or identification papers, to police. Sixty-nine people were killed and another 180 wounded when police opened fire. The incident was called the Sharpeville massacre. The world condemned the incident, as by now it had a number of other outrages by the South African government.

The black community responded with more protests. In retaliation[1], the government declared a state of emergency, which allowed authorities to further suspend the rights of blacks and make even more arrests. Again, the crackdown had just the opposite effect of what was intended. With more of its leaders in jail, the ANC had a chance to plan new actions. The group selected Mandela to lead the ANC during the next phase of the struggle.

In the treason trial, the state tried to prove that the ANC was a Communist organization, bent[2] on establishing a Communist government in South Africa. The state took several years to develop its case and racked up[3] a small fortune in legal expenses. But in the end, on March 29, 1961, the defendants were found not guilty.

特兰斯凯举行婚礼。

叛国罪审判

曼德拉夫妇度了个称不上是蜜月的蜜月，叛国罪的庭审在他们结婚的同一个月里正式开始。针对最初156名抗议者中大部分人的指控已经被驳回。但是对核心分子中30人的指控仍然成立，其中就包括曼德拉。在庭审过程中，他一直在狱中。

就在备受关注的审判进行的同时，骚乱在黑人区里继续着。1960年，在一个火车站举行的和平抗议中，一群黑人拒绝向警察出示有色人种身份证，也就是证明身份的文件。警察开火，造成69人死亡，另外180人受伤。这次事件被称为沙佩维尔大屠杀。世界对该暴力事件一片谴责，因为到这时为止，南非政府还制造了一系列其他暴行。

作为回应，黑人又发起了更多的抗议活动。作为报复，政府宣布国家进入紧急状态，允许当局临时取消黑人更多的权利，并进行更大规模的抓捕行动。同样，镇压又一次适得其反。由于更多的领袖进了监狱，非国大有机会计划新的行动。组织推举曼德拉来领导非国大下一阶段的斗争。

在叛国罪庭审中，政府试图证明非国大是共产主义团体，决心在南非建立共产主义政体。政府花了数年时间在诉讼上，通过法律费用累积取得了一小笔财富。可是到最后，在1961年3月29日，被告被宣布无罪。

[1] retaliation 报复

[2] bent 有强烈意向的

[3] racked up 累积取得

As the defendants left the courthouse they were greeted by enthusiastic crowds who cheered and sang *Nkosi Sikelel' iAfrika*. Mandela was pleased with the outcome of the trial, but he had no illusions about the future. He knew that the authorities were going to work harder next time to make sure that the activists stayed in jail.

NELSON MANDELA

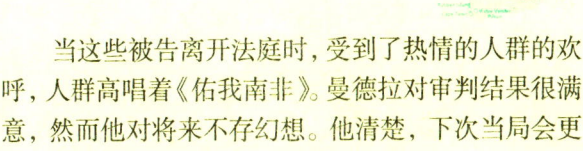

　　当这些被告离开法庭时，受到了热情的人群的欢呼，人群高唱着《佑我南非》。曼德拉对审判结果很满意，然而他对将来不存幻想。他清楚，下次当局会更狠，直至把这些激进主义分子都投进监狱。

CHAPTER SEVEN
THE BLACK PIMPERNEL

黑 海 绿

In 1961 the banning orders that had hampered[1] Mandela off and on for nearly a decade ran out. He had his public voice back, but he went underground to preserve it. With a frustrated police force frantic[2] to keep an eye on him, Mandela began the bittersweet life of a fugitive[3].

For the first time in years, he traveled to the countryside. His banning orders had restricted him to Johannesburg for so long that he had nearly forgotten the natural beauty of rural South Africa. He met with rural activists and with journalists to explain his positions and argue his points. He wrote letters to students, who were by then becoming a powerful force in the struggle.

Mandela worked closely with his old friend and mentor Walter Sisulu. Mandela later noted that the older man gave him a sense of calm that enabled him to discuss his ideas with even the harshest critics without losing his temper—or the argument.

Mandela was invisible to the authorities, but his presence was felt in nearly every part of the country. The police conducted a massive manhunt, but Mandela continued to elude[4] them. By now he and Winnie had two daughters, Zenani and Zindziswa. He visited them whenever possible, usually slipping in and out late at night. There were a few close calls, but he managed to stay one step ahead of the police.

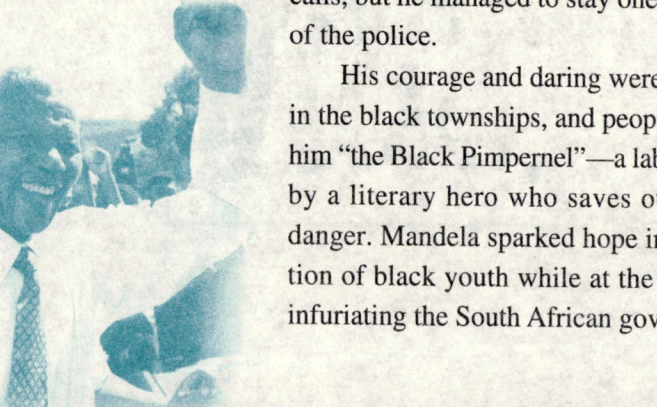

His courage and daring were legendary in the black townships, and people renamed him "the Black Pimpernel"—a label inspired by a literary hero who saves others from danger. Mandela sparked hope in a generation of black youth while at the same time infuriating the South African government.

NELSON MANDELA

纳尔逊·曼德拉

[1] hampered 妨碍

[2] frantic （因焦虑、恐惧、激动、喜悦等）发狂似的

[3] fugitive 逃亡者

[4] elude 躲避

　　1961年，断断续续妨碍曼德拉人身自由近10年的禁令终于期满了。他又获得了公开发表言论的权力，然而为了保护这种权力，他转入了地下。受到打击的警察不遗余力地对他进行监视，曼德拉开始了苦乐参半的逃亡生活。

　　数年来头一次，他旅行去了乡下。禁令将他困在约翰内斯堡如此之久，他几乎都忘了南非乡村的自然美景了。他会见了农村激进主义分子和记者，向他们解释他的立场，论证他的观点。他写信给学生们，这些学生在那时已成为斗争的强大力量。

　　曼德拉与他的良师益友瓦尔特·西苏卢紧密合作。曼德拉后来指出，这位长者给了他一种镇定感，令他哪怕在与最苛刻的评论家讨论自己的想法时也不至于发脾气——或丢掉自己的论点。

　　曼德拉并不暴露在当局的视野中，但他的存在在这个国家的几乎每一处都能被感觉到。警方展开大规模的追捕，而曼德拉总是巧妙地躲开了。到这时，他和温妮有了两个女儿，泽娜妮和金德基斯娃。无论何时，只要有可能，他就去看她们，经常是在半夜溜进溜出。有几次他差点被抓住，不过他比警察快了一步。

　　他的勇气与胆量在黑人居住区内变成了传奇，人们给他取了个绰号叫"黑海绿"——这是文学作品中一位救人于危难的英雄的绰号。曼德拉激励了年青一代的黑人，同时激怒了南非政府。

It was during this period that Mandela and a small number of ANC members formed a radical group called Umkhonto we Sizwe (Spear of the Nation). Since its establishment in 1912, the ANC had engaged in only nonviolent protests. But in situation after situation, peaceful protest had been met with police violence and further erosion of the rights of the black majority. Spear of the Nation resolved to try another tactic.

Setting up headquarters at a farm in a suburb of Johannesburg, the group decided to engage in acts of sabotage[1] against property and the economy. These actions were designed to put pressure on the government to make changes. But the leaders were careful to plan acts that would not harm people. They worked out the details of their plans during September, October, and November of 1961. Mandela lived at the farm during this period and was also able to spend some happy moments with his wife and children.

Ironically, just as the ANC was moving toward limited acts of violence, the world paid homage[2] to its nearly fifty years of nonviolence. In early December 1961, former ANC president Albert Luthuli became the first African to be awarded the Nobel Prize for Peace. Within a week, on December 16, Spear of the Nation launched bomb attacks on sites in Johannesburg, Port Elizabeth, and Durban.

One Spear of the Nation member was killed in the explosions, which rocked white South Africa to its very foundations. Finally, liberals and moderates began to listen to the problems of the black majority, while the government prepared itself for an internal war.

That same month, the ANC received an invitation to attend the Pan African Freedom Movement conference in Addis Ababa, Ethiopia. The conference would

NELSON MANDELA

在这期间，曼德拉与非国大的一小部分成员创立了激进组织"民族之矛"。从1912年成立起，非国大就一直坚持非暴力抗议形式。然而在一次又一次的事件当中，和平抗议遭遇到了警方的暴力，占多数的黑人的权利进一步受到了侵蚀。民族之矛决意尝试另一种策略。

该组织将总部设在约翰内斯堡郊区的一个农场里，组织决定对财产和经济进行秘密破坏。他们希望这些行动能给政府施加压力，从而迫使其改变现状。但是领袖们制定行动计划时很小心，以免这些行动伤及群众。在1961年的9月、10月和11月，他们确定了计划的具体细节。曼德拉在此期间都住在农场，同时也可以和妻子以及孩子们一起度过一段快乐的时光。

讽刺的是，就在非国大向有节制地使用暴力过渡的时候，世界对其将近50年坚持非暴力的宗旨表达了敬意。1961年12月初，前非国大主席艾伯特·卢图利成为第一位获得诺贝尔和平奖的非洲人。不到一周后的12月16日，民族之矛对约翰内斯堡、伊丽莎白港和德班进行了炸弹袭击。

一名民族之矛成员在爆炸中丧生，而爆炸给南非白人带来了根本性的震撼。最终，自由派和温和派人士开始倾听占多数的黑人的问题了，而政府则做好了内战的准备。

同月，非国大收到了邀请，邀请其出席在埃塞俄比亚的亚的斯亚贝巴举行的泛非自由运动大会。这次会议将把整个非洲的领导人联合

[1] sabotage 蓄意破坏，阴谋破坏（常指以破坏机器、建筑物等来打击某一企业或战时之国家）

[2] homage 敬意，尊敬

纳尔逊·曼德拉

·**111**·

unite leaders from all over Africa. The ANC decided to send Nelson Mandela as its representative. But he was not sure that he should go.

Mandela had earlier announced that he would not leave the country in such a time of danger. If African blood was to be spilled, he said, his would mingle[1] with the rest. But Albert Luthuli and the others finally convinced Mandela to go. In January 1962, he sadly said good-bye to Winnie and his children and slipped out of the country.

In addition to attending the Pan African conference, Mandela toured East, West, and North Africa like a head of state. He visited the heads of African nations that had only recently thrown off the colonial yoke. He exchanged ideas with men who would lead their countries in the years to come. He received military training in Algeria, a country that had won independence from France barely two years earlier. Other African leaders were sympathetic to Mandela's cause. Some lent financial support, while others committed themselves to training ANC members.

Mandela then traveled to England and found a number of politicians within the Labor and Liberal Parties willing to discuss the situation in South Africa. He created quite a stir wherever he traveled, and the media took notice. All the while, his opponents in Pretoria watched from afar and waited.

After roughly seven months of travel, Mandela made good[2] on his

promise not to abandon South Africa. He returned to the country of his birth. He was happy to see his family and friends again, but he was also sad. South Africa had not changed in his absence. The white government continued to brutally oppress.

Back home, the Black Pimpernel again took up the life of a hunted fugitive. By now he had become a kind of Robin Hood to

起来。非国大决定派曼德拉为代表出席会议。可是他不确定自己是否应该去。

　　曼德拉早先已经声明，他不会在如此危急的时刻离开国家。他说，如果非洲人将流血，他的鲜血就将和其他人的混合在一起。不过艾伯特·卢图利以及其他人最终说服了他前去赴会。1962 年 1 月，他悲伤地与温妮和孩子们告别，悄悄离开了这个国家。

　　除了参加泛非大会，曼德拉还访问了东非、西非和北非，就像是一位国家元首。他会见了非洲多个国家的首脑，这些国家最近才摆脱了殖民统治的枷锁。他与那些将在未来数年中领导国家的人交换了意见。他在阿尔及利亚接受了军事训练，该国两年前刚刚从法国统治下获得独立。其他非洲首脑对曼德拉的事业表示同情。一部分提供了经济援助，还有的允诺训练非国大的成员。

　　曼德拉接着来到英格兰，遇到了许多工党和自由党的政治家，他们愿意与他讨论南非的形势。他所到之处无不引起轰动，媒体频频关注。自始至终，比勒陀利亚的对手们都远远地注视着他，等待着他。

　　经过了大约 7 个月的旅行，曼德拉信守了诺言，没有抛弃南非，回到了他的祖国。他很高兴又见到了家人和朋友，但是他也很伤感。南非在他离开的期间没有任何改变。白人政府继续进行残忍的压迫。

　　回到家，"黑海绿"又过上了被搜捕的逃亡生活。到了这时，他已经成为黑人、印第安人、有色人种，甚至是那些信奉民主的白人心目中

[1] mingle　混合

[2] made good
　　实现（诺言等）

纳尔逊·曼德拉

blacks, Indians, coloreds, and even whites who believed in democracy. To the government, he was an embarrassment, an unwelcome symbol of resistance, and the most dangerous man in the country. In early August 1962, the police got a tip on where they might find Mandela, and they closed in.

Trial and Imprisonment

Mandela had become a legend. He had traveled and made connections all over the world and could have easily remained in comfortable exile. Undoubtedly, the authorities would have welcomed that. They might even have allowed his family to join him out of the country.

Yet Mandela was a different sort of leader. He recalled the history of his people and his heritage within Thembu royalty. He recalled the iron-fisted injustice for which Pretoria was famous and knew he could not save his people and himself at the same time. He would be there with them and make whatever sacrifice was necessary. After nearly seventeen months on the run, Mandela was arrested and put in a prison called the Johannesburg Fort. He was charged with inciting[1] people to strike and with leaving the country illegally.

South Africa's minister of justice during that time was John Vorster, a man who had been jailed during World War II for his pro-Nazi views.

During his term in office, he greatly limited freedom of speech and protest. He also helped pass the Sabotage Act, increasing penalties for trespassing[2], illegal possession of weapons, and other crimes. The minister also made banning more severe. Under the new laws, a banned person could not publish writings, receive visitors, or broadcast statements. Banned people had to report regularly to the police.

罗宾汉式的人物。对于政府来说，他是种难堪，是不受欢迎的抵抗的象征，也是整个国家里最危险的人物。1962年8月初，警方接到消息说能在某地找到曼德拉，他们立刻封锁了该地。

审判与入狱

曼德拉已成为一个传奇。他已访问并与世界各地建立了联系，可以很容易地选择舒适的流亡生活。毫无疑问，当权者会很欢迎他那样做，他们甚至可能会允许其家人也离境与他团聚。

然而，曼德拉是位不同寻常的领袖，他牢记着自己人民的历史与坦布王室内的传统，他牢记着比勒陀利亚臭名昭著的铁拳下的不公正。他明白自己无法同时拯救人民和他自己。他要与他们在一起，作任何必要的牺牲。逃亡了近17个月之后，曼德拉被捕，被关进了名叫"约翰内斯堡福特"的监狱。他被控煽动群众罢工以及非法离境。

当时的南非司法部长是约翰·沃斯特，此人在第二次世界大战中由于亲纳粹的立场而入狱。他担任司法部长时，严格限制言论自由以及抗议活动。他还帮助通过了《破坏法》，严惩非法侵入、非法拥有武器以及其他罪行。此位部长还进一步加强了禁令的力度。新法律规定，受到禁令者不能发表文章，不能会见访客，不能广播声明。受到禁令者必须定期向警方报到。

[1] inciting 鼓动；
煽动

[2] trespassing
非法侵入

纳尔逊·曼德拉

As restrictions tightened within South Africa, criticism of apartheid mounted on a global scale. The world had begun to condemn South Africa, and its government felt like it was under siege[1]. It became defensive and prepared to do battle. Mandela was the symbol of a new national threat, and the government seemed determined to deal with him as such.

At the hearing following his arrest, Mandela noticed many familiar faces in the courtroom. He knew the judge and some of the lawyers from his years of practicing law. He also noticed that they seemed uneasy, even ashamed, when the hearing started. Here he was, labeled the most dangerous and wanted fugitive in South Africa—an outlaw of the highest order—but the lawyers treated him with professional courtesy and respect. He was Nelson Mandela, attorney-at-law, as far as they were concerned. It dawned on Mandela that these people saw him as an ordinary man being punished for his beliefs—beliefs that they knew to be honorable.

With that revelation, Mandela shook off the depression he had felt over his loss of freedom. He began to see that the world perceived him as a symbol of justice in the court of a tyrant. This feeling would grow in the coming weeks leading up to the actual trial.

NELSON MANDELA

Mandela planned to conduct his own defense. But he also enlisted the help of lawyer and Communist Party member Joe Slovo in preparing his case. Then, the trial was moved to Pretoria, and Slovo had to be replaced. A banning order restricted him to Johannesburg.

On October 15, 1962, Mandela's trial began in Pretoria. The guardians of the old order felt they finally had him where they wanted him. They thought they would silence

就在南非加强限制的同时，对种族隔离的批评遍及全球。整个世界都开始谴责南非，政府感到自己四面楚歌。它开始采取防守措施，做好了搏斗的准备。曼德拉是新的国家威胁的象征，政府似乎打定主意就要以此治他的罪。

在被捕后的听证会上，曼德拉在法庭见到很多熟悉的面孔。他见到的法官以及几名律师是他在做律师的那些年认识的。他还注意到他们在听证会开始时显得不安，甚至面露愧色。他站在这里，被称为南非最危险的通缉犯——最高级别的逃犯——但是律师们都以职业的礼节与尊重对待他。对他们而言，他是曼德拉，是位律师。曼德拉意识到这些人把他看做是因坚持信念而受到惩罚的普通人——他们也知道这信念是高尚的。

明白了这些，曼德拉摆脱了失去自由的沮丧，他开始明白，世界已将他看做暴君法庭中正义的象征。这种感觉将在未来数周内愈发强烈，直到判决的来临。

曼德拉计划为自己辩护，但他还是请律师、共产党员乔·斯洛沃帮助他准备案子。后来，庭审被移至比勒陀利亚进行，斯洛沃不得不被替换，禁令限制他离开约翰内斯堡。

1962年10月15日，曼德拉的庭审在比勒陀利亚开始。旧秩序的卫道士们感觉他们终于如愿将他送至他们希望的地方了。他们认为他们将让他闭嘴，羞

[1] siege　围攻；
　　包围

纳尔逊·曼德拉

him, humble him, and ultimately break him.

But the old freedom fighter had something else in mind. Had the authorities forgotten that he was a lawyer who thrived[1] on trials? He was exactly where he needed to be. Throngs[2] of supporters and journalists gathered from around the world. Everyone sensed that something monumental was about to take place, but few would have predicted what they were about to see.

As the trial opened, Mandela strode[3] proudly into the packed Pretoria courtroom wearing a traditional Xhosa leopard-skin kaross[4], or cape[5], an outfit he would wear throughout the trial. He looked like a Xhosa king walking into a royal kraal for a coronation.

"*Amandla*" ("Power"), someone shouted and thrust a clenched fist into the air. "*Ngawethu*" ("The power is ours"), another voice intoned. Then, nearly everyone in the gallery rose and chanted until the pounding of the magistrate's gavel[6] silenced them. Winnie was among them. She was also dressed in Xhosa attire[7], which brought a smile to her husband's face.

Nelson Mandela wanted the world to know that this was not the trial of one man. He was not alone. Accompanying him into the courtroom were the ancestors of the freedom movement. Although invisible to the judge and guards, Mandela felt their presence. Xhosa King

Ngangelizwe, who had fought the British in the nineteenth century, was there. Beside him walked Sekhukhne, king of the Bapedi; Moshoeshoe, the Basotho king; and Dingane, king of the Zulu. Their courage flowed through Mandela as he went to do battle in the way he knew best. He would use the trial to air grievances[8] that were decades, if not centuries, old. Mandela intended to put the

辱他，并最终击垮他。

但是，这个久经考验的自由战士脑子里还有别的想法。当权者难道忘了，他自己就是一名通过各种审讯案件茁壮成长的律师吗？这个地方对他来说正合适。支持者和记者从世界各地蜂拥而至。每个人都意识到将要发生意义重大的事件，然而很少有人能预见到他们将要看到的事情。

当庭审开始时，曼德拉充满自豪地阔步走进拥挤的比勒陀利亚法庭，身着科萨部落的传统豹皮斗篷，也就是披肩，他将在整个庭审过程中一直穿着这套衣服。他看上去像一位科萨首领来到王室村庄参加加冕典礼。

"力量"，有人大叫，并在空中挥舞着捏紧的拳头。"力量属于我们"，另一个声音吟诵道。继而，几乎现场的所有人都站了起来，不断吟诵，直到法官的木槌敲响才安静下来。温妮也在人群里，她也同样身着科萨服装，这使她丈夫脸上浮现出一丝笑容。

纳尔逊·曼德拉要让世界知道，这不仅仅是对一个人的审判。他并不是一个人。陪伴他进入法庭的是那些自由运动的先驱。虽然那些法官和警卫看不见，但曼德拉能够感知他们的存在。19世纪抗击英军的科萨首领恩冈基兹维在那里，走在他旁边的是巴佩迪的首领萨科胡克尼、巴苏陀的首领莫舒舒，还有祖鲁的首领丁冈。先驱们的勇气传给了曼德拉，他用他所知道的最好的方式去战斗。他要利用这次审判将那已持续了几十年(如果说不是几百年的话)的不平等昭然于天下。曼德拉意欲将这个国家本身推上

[1] thrived 茁壮成长
[2] Throngs 群，群众
[3] strode 大踏步走
[4] kaross (南非土人穿的)毛皮斗篷(或坎肩)，毛皮毯
[5] cape 斗篷，披肩
[6] gavel 木槌
[7] attire 服装

[8] grievances 委屈；冤情

纳尔逊 · 曼德拉

country itself on trial.

The battle did not actually begin that day. Mandela requested and was granted more time to prepare his case. He had thrown down the gauntlet[1], but it would be a week before an actual exchange would take place.

Mandela returned to court on October 22, 1962, and immediately took the offensive. He called for the judge to excuse himself from the case on the grounds that he was biased against the defendant. In fact, Mandela questioned whether the court had the right to hear the case at all. After all, as a black man, Mandela had no representative or voice in the South African government. He asked how that same government could expect him to abide by its laws. He went on to outline the rights that whites monopolized[2]. He pointed out numerous ways in which blacks were kept on the bottom of society. In such an atmosphere, he questioned whether the court could give him a fair trial:

Why is it that in this courtroom I am facing a white magistrate, confronted by a white prosecutor[3], escorted by white orderlies? Can anybody honestly and seriously suggest that in this type of atmosphere the scales of justice are evenly balanced? Why is it that no African in the history of this country has ever had the honor of being tried by his own kind, by his own flesh and blood?...I am a black man in a white man's court. This should not be.

The judge remained unpersuaded and ordered the case to move forward.

The prosecutor, Bob Bosch, was another lawyer who respected Mandela for his previous legal work. Nonetheless, he presented a vigorous case, calling more than one hundred witnesses. Mandela was no less aggressive as he questioned the witnesses

审判台。

那一天战斗还没有真正打响。曼德拉要求并获准用更多的时间为案子做准备。他已提出了挑战，但真正的交锋将在一周后开始。

曼德拉于 1962 年 10 月 22 日回到法庭，并立即采取主动进攻。他要求法官回避审理此案，因为他对被告存有偏见。事实上，曼德拉质疑法庭是否有资格审理此案。毕竟，作为一名黑人，曼德拉在南非政府中没有代表，也没有发言权。他质问，这样的一个政府，怎么能期望他去遵守它的法律。他继续概述了白人独占的种种权利。他指出无数将黑人打压在社会底层的手段。在这样的气氛下，他质疑法庭是否能给他公正的裁决：

为何在这个法庭上，我面对的是白人法官，与白人起诉人对质，押送我的是白人卫兵？有没有哪个人能诚实、严肃地说，在这样的氛围中，公正的天平依然是水平的？为何在这个国家的历史上，没有一个非洲人有幸受到自己种族、自己同胞的审判？……我是在白人法庭上的黑人。这可不行。

法官不为所动，命令庭审继续进行。

起诉人鲍勃·伯什也是一名律师，他对曼德拉从前从事的法律工作颇感敬佩。虽然如此，他举出了有力的证据，传唤了 100 多名证人。曼德拉在对证人们的盘问

[1] thrown down the gauntlet
（把带护甲手套扔地上表示）挑战

[2] monopolized
垄断；独占

[3] prosecutor 起诉人

纳尔逊·曼德拉

on cross-examination[1]. He pressed them hard, which often resulted in tense exchanges. But by the time the prosecution rested, there was strong evidence to show that Mandela had indeed left the country illegally and had incited workers to strike.

It was then the defense's turn to present its case. Surprisingly, Mandela announced that he would call no witnesses. He further announced he was resting his case. The judge, prosecutor, and spectators were shocked, and whispers rippled[2] through the gallery[3]. The prosecutor fumbled[4] for words. He had not expected to present his closing argument so quickly. Finally, he simply asked the court to find the defendant guilty on both counts, and the court went into a short recess.

It was during the recess that prosecutor Bosch paid Mandela a surprise visit. Bosch apologized to him, explaining that he hated what he was doing, hated having to send Mandela to prison. Bosch then extended his hand. It is likely that most people in that situation would have given the prosecutor a piece of their mind[5]. Mandela, however, accepted the handshake and thanked Bosch for his words.

When the court session[6] began again, the judge summed up the charges and asked if Mandela had any closing remarks. He certainly did—he spoke for nearly an hour. He never denied that he had traveled outside the country without the government's permission. He never denied encouraging blacks to boycott work during the 1961 campaigns. But he maintained that he wasn't a criminal. "I have done my duty to my people and to South Africa," he said. "I have no doubt that posterity[7] will pronounce that I was innocent and that the criminals that should have been brought before this court are the members of the government."

NELSON MANDELA

[1] cross-examina-
tion （尤指对
对方证人的）盘
问

[2] rippled 波及
开去，荡漾开来
[3] gallery （高尔
夫球、网球等体
育比赛或立法
会议等的）观
众；听众；公众
[4] fumbled （为
寻找东西）笨拙
地摸索
[5] given a piece of
their mind 斥
责，坦白告诉某
人对他的看法
[6] session 开庭

[7] posterity 后代

中毫不示弱。他极力向他们施压，以至于总是弄得剑拔弩张。但到休庭时为止，有强有力的证据表明，曼德拉的确曾非法离境，并煽动工人们进行罢工。

接下去轮到辩方举证了。令人吃惊的是，曼德拉宣布将不传唤任何证人。他甚至宣布将停止辩护。法官、起诉人和观众全惊呆了，观众窃窃私语。起诉人苦苦思索着该说的话。他没有预料到这么快就进入总结陈词的阶段。最后，他只要求法庭判处被告两项罪名成立，法庭随即短暂休庭。

就在休庭时，起诉人伯什出人意料地来找曼德拉。伯什向他道歉，解释说他痛恨自己所做的事，痛恨必须将曼德拉送进监狱。伯什然后伸出手。似乎大多数人在那样的情景下都会斥责起诉人。然而，曼德拉和伯什握了手，并对他的话表示感谢。

庭审再次开始，法官对全部指控进行了总结，问曼德拉最后是否还有话要说。他当然有——他说了将近一个小时。他从未否认自己在未经政府允许的情况下擅自离开国家。他从未否认在1961年的运动中鼓励黑人罢工。但是他坚持认为自己不是罪犯。"我已为我的人民，为南非尽了责任，"他说。"我毫不怀疑，子孙后代会宣告我的无辜，会宣告真正应该被带到这个法庭前的罪犯是那些政府的人。"

·*123*·

Ten minutes later, following another recess to consider the sentence, the judge returned and pronounced a sentence of five years in prison: three years for inciting people to strike and two years for leaving the country. In Port Elizabeth, acts of sabotage greeted the news of the conviction.

A day earlier, on November 6, 1962, the General Assembly of the United Nations had voted in favor of sanctions, or penalties, against South Africa for its human rights abuses. Some countries refused to do business with South Africa. They hoped to hurt South Africa economically as a way to pressure the government to make changes.

Mandela was to serve five years without the possibility of parole[1]. This was a harsh sentence, and some people in the courtroom responded with wails and weeping. Without knowing for sure, Mandela felt Winnie must have been among them. The punishment would hurt her almost as much as him. Still, Mandela stood tall and proud. He raised a clenched fist to the gallery, and the crowd roared: "*Amandla! Amandla! Amandla!*"

The fervor of the crowd's response confirmed Mandela's feeling that his personal sacrifices were worth it. He was filled with a sense of love for the African people and all those who struggled to end the nightmare of apartheid. But what moved him to tears was the singing of the South African national anthem, *Nkosi Sikelel' iAfrika.*

Following the reading of the sentence, Winnie and her husband had only a few minutes to say good-bye. Despite the anguish[2] she was feeling, she wore a brave face. There were no tears. She never lost sight of the fact that she was also a comrade in the struggle.

As Mandela was taken away in a police van, he heard the crowd of supporters singing *Nkosi Sikelel' iAfrika* in his honor. He

休庭10分钟后，法官考虑好了对曼德拉的判决，他回到法庭宣布判处曼德拉5年监禁：因鼓动人民罢工被判处3年监禁，因擅离国家被判处2年监禁。在伊丽莎白港，作为对判决的回应，发生了多起破坏事件。

就在一天以前的1962年11月6日，由于南非对人权的摧残，联合国大会已经投票通过了对南非的制裁（即处罚）决定。部分国家拒绝与南非进行商业合作。他们试图通过打击南非经济迫使其政府做出改变。

[1] parole 假释

曼德拉被判5年徒刑，不得假释。这是相当严厉的判决，法庭里的一些群众号啕大哭。虽然无法确定，但曼德拉感觉温妮肯定也哭了。这项惩罚对她的打击丝毫不亚于对他自己的打击。尽管如此，曼德拉依然高傲地昂首站立着。他攥紧拳头挥向观众，人群大叫："力量！力量！力量！"

群众热烈的回应证明了曼德拉的感觉是对的，即他个人的牺牲是值得的。他的心中充溢着对非洲人民和所有那些为终结种族隔离梦魇而斗争的人民的热爱之情。然而使他感动落泪的是人们高唱南非国歌《佑我南非》。

[2] anguish 痛苦

判决宣布以后，温妮只有几分钟的时间与丈夫告别。尽管内心备受煎熬，她仍保持着勇敢的神情。没有眼泪。她从没忘记，自己也是斗争的一分子。

当曼德拉将被警车带走时，他听到支持者的人群高唱《佑我南非》，以向他表示

纳尔逊·曼德拉

held the face of Winnie in his mind and his spirits soared. However, soon other faces came to mind: his young children, Zenani and Zindziswa, as well as Thembelike and Makgatho from his first marriage. His longing for them was enough to make him weep.

Mandela went first to Pretoria Central Prison, but within a short time he was transferred to the notorious Robbens Island. The Island, as it was often called, was all too familiar to the Xhosa. The windswept rock, four miles off the coast of Cape Town, had been used as a prison since the Boers settled in Africa in the seventeenth century. The prison was set up to break the spirits of those who resisted the rule of the state.

Although there were white prisoners on the island, the worst treatment was reserved for black prisoners, especially those convicted of political crimes. Mandela's clothes were confiscated[1], and he was issued the standard attire for African prisoners: a pair of baggy shorts, a prison shirt, and sandals[2]. He and the other African prisoners were not allowed to wear long pants like white prisoners, even in winter when the temperature often dipped below freezing. By dressing the black prisoners like children, the state meant to remind them that it indeed thought of blacks as such.

Some months after his arrival on the Island, Mandela was transferred back to Pretoria. He soon learned through the prison grapevine[3] that other

members of the ANC had been arrested and awaited trial on charges of sabotage for the Spear of the Nation bombings. The government wasted no time in blaming Mandela and charging him with sabotage, too.

The State versus Nelson Mandela and others was to be argued before the Supreme Court in the South African Palace of Justice. Not far from the entrance to the palace stood

敬意。他的脑海中刻进了温妮的面容，情绪
高涨。然而，他很快又想起其他一些面容：他
的孩子们，泽娜妮和金德基斯娃，还有第一
次婚姻留下的孩子，坦贝莱克和马加托。对
他们的思念足以使他流泪。

曼德拉首先被关进比勒陀利亚中央监狱，
但不久后就被转到了臭名昭著的罗本岛。这
个经常被称为"岛"的地方，对于科萨人来
说再熟悉不过了。这块受风侵袭的岩石距离
开普敦海岸有4英里，从17世纪布尔人登陆非
洲时就开始被用作监狱了。这个监狱是专门
为击垮那些抵抗国家统治的人而建立的。

虽然岛上也有白人囚犯，但是最恶劣的
手段都是留给黑人囚犯的，尤其是那些政治
犯。曼德拉的衣服被收缴，再被分发了供非洲
因犯穿的标准服装：一条肥大的短裤，一件囚
衣，外加一双凉鞋。他和其他非洲囚犯都不被
允许像白人囚犯那样穿长裤，就算是在气温
经常降到零度以下的冬天也一样。当局把黑
人囚犯打扮成小孩的样子，就是为了要提醒
他们，在国家的心目中他们就是这样的。

在岛上度过了几个月后，曼德拉被转回
到比勒陀利亚。他很快听到监狱里的谣言，说
又有几名非国大的领导人被捕了，他们因民
族之矛策划的一系列炸弹袭击事件而受到指
控，现正等待审判。政府立刻把破坏事件同时
归咎于曼德拉，并指控他犯有相同的罪名。

"国家讼纳尔逊·曼德拉等人"的案
件将在位于南非司法大楼内的最高法
院进行审判。距离大楼入口不远处立着

[1] confiscated
没收

[2] sandals 凉鞋

[3] grapevine （内
幕消息、谣言等
的）传播途径

纳尔逊·曼德拉

a statue of Paul Kruger, an Afrikaner founding father who fought against British rule in the nineteenth century. There was an inscription on the pedestal[1] that read:

In confidence we lay our cause before the world. Whether we win or die, freedom will rise in Africa like the sun from the morning clouds.

How things had changed. The once oppressed Afrikaners had become the oppressors. Still, as the police transport passed the statue, Mandela considered just how appropriate the words were for the struggle of blacks in his country.

I Am the First Accused

"I am the first accused," Nelson Mandela said in his first public statement in over a year. It was the beginning of a lengthy statement that introduced the defense's case in the sabotage trial of April 1964.

Mandela explained that Spear of the Nation felt it had no course other than violent action. "All lawful modes of expressing opposition to this principle [apartheid] had been closed by legislation, and we were placed in a position in which we had either to accept a permanent state of inferiority[2], or defy the government," he said.

He went on to outline the history of the African National Congress. He explained how the ANC had first tried to work within the established

political system, noting that even after basic rights had been stripped from black people, the ANC retained its nonviolent stance. He quoted Chief Albert Luthuli who had said:

Who will deny that thirty years of my life have been spent knocking in vain, patiently, moderately, and modestly at a closed and barred door? What have been the fruits of moderation? The past thirty years

保罗·克鲁格的雕像，他是布尔人的开国者，在 19 世纪抗击英国统治。基座上刻着这样的文字：

我们用自信向世界展示理想。无论我们活着还是死去，自由将如早晨从云中升起的太阳一样在非洲升起。

世道变化如此之大。曾经被压迫的布尔人如今成了压迫者。尽管如此，当警车从雕像前经过时，曼德拉感到那上面的文字对于自己国家的黑人斗争是如此的恰如其分。

我是第一被告

"我是第一被告，"纳尔逊·曼德拉在时隔一年多的第一次公开声明中说了这句话。在对 1964 年 4 月破坏事件的审判中，这是辩方举证前漫长陈述的开始。

曼德拉辩护说，民族之矛认为除了暴力行动外已经别无他法。"所有合法反对该制度（种族隔离制度）的途径都已经为立法所封堵。我们被置于一种境地，要么永远接受劣等公民的身份，要么反抗政府，"他说。

他继而略述了非洲人国民大会的历史。他解释了非国大如何在一开始试图在既定政治体系内开展工作，指出甚至在黑人的基本权利被剥夺后，非国大仍坚持其非暴力的立场。他引用艾伯特·卢图利主席的话说：

谁能否认，我生命的 30 年都用在徒劳地、耐心地、节制地、谨慎地敲着一扇始终紧闭、禁止入内的大门上了？节制的后果是什么？在过去 30 年中所产生的

[1] pedestal 基座

[2] inferiority 下等；劣等

have seen the greatest number of laws restricting our rights and progress, until today we have reached a stage where we have almost no rights.

Mandela explained that in 1949, the ANC had shifted its tactics somewhat, launching a Defiance Campaign of demonstrations and labor strikes. Although nearly 9,000 people had gone to jail during the campaign, it had remained nonviolent. And while the ANC had maintained its commitment to peaceful demonstrations over the years, the government had launched countless acts of violence against the people. Mandela continued before the judge:

Already, scores of Africans had died as a result of racial friction. In 1920 when the famous leader Masabala was held in Port Elizabeth jail, twenty-four of a group of Africans who had gathered to demand his release were killed by police and white civilians. In 1921, more than one hundred Africans died in the Bulhoek affair. In 1924 over two hundred Africans were killed when the Administrator of South-West Africa led a force against a group which had rebelled against the imposition of a dog tax. On May 1, 1950, eighteen Africans died as a result of police shootings during the strike. On March 21, 1960, sixty-nine unarmed Africans died at Sharpeville. How many more Sharpevilles would there be?...The hard facts were that fifty years of nonviolence had brought the African people nothing but more and more repressive legislation, and fewer and fewer

rights....It showed that a Government which uses force to maintain its rule teaches the oppressed to use force to oppose it.

Mandela's voice filled the courtroom as he laid out what most of white South Africa had never contemplated. He explained that the ANC leadership had agonized[1] over how to proceed after nonviolent tactics had failed. They had begun to discuss their options, and

限制我们权利与进步的新法律是如此之多，直
到如今，我们到了几乎没有任何权利的境地。

曼德拉辩护说，非国大在1949年对
其政策进行了一定的调整，推行由示威和
罢工组成的蔑视运动。尽管有将近9 000
人在运动期间被捕入狱，它仍然坚持非暴
力的宗旨。在非国大数年来始终坚持其和
平示威承诺的同时，政府却制造了无数起
针对人民的暴力事件。曼德拉面对法官继
续说：

已经有无数非洲人死于种族冲突。1920
年，著名领袖马萨巴拉被关进伊丽莎白港监
狱，24名非洲人进行集会，要求释放马萨巴
拉，他们被警察和白人平民杀害。1921年，
100多名非洲人死于布尔霍克事件。1924年，
西南非当局武力镇压反对实施一项有关狗的
税收的团体，超过200名非洲人被杀害。1950
年5月1日，18名非洲人在罢工期间遭警察
射杀。1960年3月21日，69名赤手空拳的非
洲人在沙佩维尔遇害。沙佩维尔惨案到底还
要再发生多少次？……残酷的现实是，50年
的非暴力主张给非洲人民带来的只是更加具
有压制性的立法，以及越来越少的权
利。……这一切证明，一个用暴力维护其统
治的政府教会了受压迫的人们以暴制暴。

曼德拉的声音响彻法庭，他揭示了
大多数南非白人从未思考过的问题。他
辩护说，在非暴力策略失败后，非国大领
导层为下一步的行动而苦苦思索了许久。
他们讨论了可供选择的办法，之后组建

[1] agonized　许
久地苦苦思索

out of that discussion they had formed Spear of the Nation. He quoted the group's manifesto[1]:

The time comes in the life of any nation when there remain only two choices—submit or fight. That time has now come to South Africa. We shall not submit and we have no choice but to hit back by all the means in our power in defense of our people, our future, and our freedom.

Mandela explained that Spear of the Nation had chosen to commit sabotage—but sabotage that would cause no loss of life. He concluded:

During my lifetime I have dedicated myself to this struggle of the African people. I have fought against white domination, and I have fought against black domination. I cherished[2] the ideal of a democratic and free society in which all persons live together in harmony and with equal opportunities. It is an ideal which I hope to live for and to achieve. But if needs be, it is an ideal for which I am prepared to die.

Mandela was eventually found guilty of four counts of sabotage and was sentenced to life in prison along with ANC members Walter Sisulu, Govan Mbeki, Raymond Mhlaba, Elias Motsoaledi, Andrew Mlangeni, Ahmed Kathrada, and Denis Goldberg.

Behind Bars

Now that Mandela was in the belly of the beast, the government set

out to accomplish two things. It would break his spirit and stamp out his memory. Once Mandela was out of circulation, the government figured people would become disheartened and forget about him.

But he was not so easily forgotten. Many grieved his imprisonment but none more than his wife, who was left to explain things to the children and to hold the family together.

NELSON MANDELA

了民族之矛。他引用组织的宣言说：

> 任何民族的生存都会遇到仅剩两种选择的时刻——屈服或战斗。这个时刻对南非来说已经到来。我们决不屈服，我们只能选择用我们所能采用的一切手段，捍卫我们的人民、我们的未来、我们的自由。

曼德拉辩护说，民族之矛选择了进行破坏活动——但破坏活动不会造成人员伤亡。他总结说：

> 我的生命已奉献给非洲人民的斗争。我对抗白人专政，也对抗黑人专政。我怀抱着民主和自由社会的理想，在那样一个社会中，所有人都可以一起和谐地生活，都有平等的机会。它是我希望能为之奋斗一生并实现的理想。然而，如果需要的话，它也是我准备为之献出生命的理想。

最终，曼德拉4项破坏活动的罪名成立，与其他几名非国大成员一起被判终身监禁，他们包括瓦尔特·西苏卢、戈文·姆贝基、雷蒙德·姆赫拉巴、伊利亚斯·莫特索阿莱迪、安德鲁·姆兰基尼、艾哈迈德·卡斯拉达和丹尼斯·戈尔德伯格。

铁窗之内

既然曼德拉成了野兽的腹中餐，政府就开始为达到两个目的而行动。政府想摧垮他的意志，并消除人们对他的记忆。一旦曼德拉离开了公众视线，政府认为人们将失去信心，并将他遗忘。

然而，他不是那么容易就会被忘记的。许多人为他的入狱感到难过，但最伤心的是他的妻子，她一个人要给孩子们解释他们面临的境况，还要使家庭保持团结。

[1] manifesto　宣言

[2] cherished　怀有，抱有（希望等）

纳尔逊·曼德拉

But Winnie knew that most black South African women faced similar burdens.

"Insofar[1] as the black woman in South Africa is concerned, each black home is a political institution," Winnie later said. "There isn't a fiber of a black's life that is not intruded upon by the apartheid laws which are so brutal that they affect little children....In our sick society, when a man hasn't been to prison, you look twice at that black man. It means that there is something wrong with that man."

Year after year, Mandela survived the rigors[2] of prison life. Through most of it, Walter Sisulu was there enduring with him. Despite the hardships, Mandela kept up a routine of physical exercise—running in place[3], sit-ups, and push-ups. He kept his mind sharp through study and, when possible, discussion. Even within the prison walls, news from the outside seeped in, and Mandela kept abreast of[4] it.

The treatment of blacks in prison continued to resemble the treatment of blacks in the rest of society. White prisoners wore long pants while blacks wore shorts. Medical care and the quality of food differed substantially for blacks and whites, as well. Over time, conditions improved, but only as a result of prisoner hunger strikes, work slowdowns, and international pressure. Eventually, black prisoners won the right to talk to one another and to have improved food, long pants, and more blankets.

NELSON MANDELA

The world had not forgotten about the freedom fighters held in captivity[5]. Mandela's name became a rallying cry[6], and the social storm intensified. Brutal police attacks were commonplace, and the black townships became ungovernable. But the government refused to change course. With every new sign of unrest, the police cracked down with no

[1] insofar 在……的范围内

[2] rigors 艰苦，严酷

[3] in place 在合适的（或常处的、原来的、指定的）位置

[4] kept abreast of 了解……的最新情况

[5] captivity 囚禁

[6] rallying cry （起号召作用的）战斗口号

不过，温妮知道南非大多数黑人妇女都面临着类似的负担。

"就南非的黑人妇女而言，每一个黑人家庭都是一个政治机构，"温妮后来说。"黑人生活的每一方面无不遭到种族隔离法的干扰，那些法律是如此残忍，连儿童也不放过……在我们病态的社会，如果一个男人没进过监狱，你倒会多看这个黑人几眼了。这说明他有不对劲的地方。"

年复一年，曼德拉在严酷的牢狱生活中生存下来。在大多数时间里，瓦尔特·西苏卢都和他共同忍耐。尽管生活艰难，曼德拉还是保持日常体育锻炼——在合适的地方跑步，做仰卧起坐和俯卧撑。他通过学习和讨论（当有可能时）保持思维的敏锐。即便在高墙之内，外界的新闻仍会传进来，曼德拉及时了解这些新闻。

黑人在监狱里也和他们在社会上的境遇相类似。白人囚犯穿长裤而黑人只能穿短裤。医疗及食物质量对于黑人和白人也有着很大差别。随着时间的推移，情况有所改善，不过这是因犯绝食抗议、怠工以及国际压力的结果。最终，黑人囚犯得到互相交谈的权利，伙食改善了，有了长裤和更多的毯子。

世界没有忘记这些陷身囹圄的自由斗士。曼德拉的名字成了战斗口号，社会更加动荡。警察的野蛮袭击司空见惯，黑人聚居地难以治理。但政府仍拒绝改变政策。一旦有新骚乱的迹象，警方就立刻镇

concern for the truth.

By the mid-1970s, black students had stepped into the forefront of the struggle. Their work was similar to the student protests in the United States during the late 1960s and early 1970s. But unlike the U.S. government, the South African government treated protesters like enemies of the state.

Things came to a tragic head in 1976 when Afrikaans, the hated language of the Boers, became a required course in South African schools. Students at all levels reacted by boycotting school. The largest boycott took place in the Soweto township outside Johannesburg.

Protests began peacefully, but the government took its usual stance of tolerating no defiance. The police moved in on the township during what came to be called the Soweto uprising. During sixteen months of unrest, roughly one thousand people died and four thousand were injured. Most of those killed and injured were children. Thousands of students were jailed. Some spent up to five years in confinement, while others were never heard from again.

The reign of terror continued the next year. So did the resistance—especially as the notion of "Black Power" filtered in from civil rights activists in the United States. As quickly as the authorities could destroy one student leader, another would move to the forefront. The best-known

student activist was Steven Biko. He was beaten to death in police custody[1]. A young Indian named Ahmed Timol was killed in a fall from the tenth floor of police headquarters in Johannesburg. Other student leaders died mysteriously, while those who survived were hampered by banning orders.

All the while, the international community increased pressure on Pretoria. Many

NELSON MANDELA

压，不分青红皂白。

到了20世纪70年代中期，黑人学生已站到了斗争的最前线。他们的斗争方式与美国20世纪60年代晚期至70年代早期发生的学生抗议活动相似。但与美国政府不同，南非政府将抗议者当成国家公敌对待。

事态在1976年达到了悲剧的顶点。当时，南非荷兰语——被憎恨的布尔人的语言——成了南非学校的一门必修课。各个年级的学生纷纷以罢课作为回应。规模最大的抵制活动发生在约翰内斯堡外的索韦托黑人区。

抗议以和平方式开始，但政府仍采取决不容忍反抗的态度。在后来被称为索韦托起义的整个过程中，警察源源不断地进入该黑人区。在16个月的骚乱过程中，大约有1 000人丧生，4 000人受伤，死伤者大多为儿童。数千名学生被捕入狱，其中一部分人被判5年监禁，而另一些人则从此杳无音讯。

第二年，恐怖统治在继续，抵抗也没有停下——尤其在"黑人权力"的思想由美国的公民权利激进主义分子传入南非后。政府刚刚打倒一名学生领袖，另一名就马上站了出来。最著名的一位学生激进主义分子是斯蒂文·比科。他在被警方羁押期间被殴打致死。一个名叫阿迈德·提穆尔的印第安青年从位于约翰内斯堡的警察总部10楼坠楼身亡。另一些学生领袖神秘死亡，而幸存下来的也受到禁令的限制。

国际社会一直在增加对比勒陀利亚的压力。

[1] custody　拘留

countries stepped up economic boycotts of South Africa, refusing to invest in South African companies or buy South African products. Since 1964, South Africa had been banned from the Olympics and other international competitions. The United Nations continued to condemn apartheid.

Bit by bit, it became apparent to the South African government that something had to be done. It was obvious that the one man capable of resolving the situation sat in prison for life. The only sane[1] course seemed to be the release of Nelson Mandela from prison and the opening of the political process to all South Africans. However, it would take the right leader to bring about the change.

NELSON MANDELA

许多国家进一步对南非实行经济抵制，拒绝投资南非
企业，也不购买南非产品。从1964年起，南非被禁止
参加奥林匹克运动会以及其他国际竞赛。联合国继续
谴责其种族隔离制度。

　　渐渐地，南非政府明显感到必须做出某些改变
了。很明显，那个可以解决当前问题的人正在狱中度
过余生。唯一明智的做法看来只能是释放纳尔逊·曼
德拉，并且赋予所有南非人政治权利。然而，需要有
一名合适的领袖才能促成这样的改变。

[1] sane　明智的

纳尔逊·曼德拉

CHAPTER EIGHT

FREE AT LAST

终于自由了

NELSON MANDELA

On July 4, 1989, while Americans celebrated Independence Day, Nelson Mandela was informed by prison officials that he was to meet with the South African president, P. W. Botha, the next day. Realizing that Mandela in prison was as much a political force as he was outside, earlier administrations had tried several times to get him out— if they could only get him to do their bidding[1]. They had pressured Mandela to renounce[2] the use of violence and illegal protests. Time and again, however, Mandela had found the government's terms unacceptable and had elected to remain in prison. He wondered if things would be different this time.

Known to have a fierce temper, President Botha was nicknamed "the Great Crocodile." He was more inclined to dictate to black leaders than to talk with them. So Mandela was surprised that the meeting turned out to be a friendly one. The two men spent much of the time discussing South African history, though from very different points of view. Finally, Mandela directed the conversation to more important matters. He explained that there could be no real negotiations until political prisoners were released unconditionally.

Not surprisingly, Botha informed Mandela that the government could  not meet his terms. In fact, the meeting ended with no real resolution. Nonetheless, Mandela felt good about it. He realized that all the pressure and social unrest were finally taking their toll[3]. It would be only a short time before his dream of a new South Africa would become a reality.

Things became less certain, however, when Botha resigned from office a month

1989 年 7 月 4 日，当美国人在庆祝独立日时，监狱官员通知纳尔逊·曼德拉，他将与南非总统博塔见面，时间就在第二天。无论曼德拉是否在狱中，他都具有相当的政治影响力，意识到这一点后，早期几届政府几次试图把他放出去———如果他们能让他只按他们的命令行事。他们向曼德拉施压，要他放弃使用暴力以及其他非法抗议手段。然而，一次又一次，曼德拉都发现政府的条件让人无法接受，于是选择了继续呆在狱中。他想知道这一次会不会有什么不同。

由于脾气十分暴躁，博塔总统的绰号是"大鳄鱼"。他更倾向于对黑人领袖们发号施令而不是和他们交谈。所以曼德拉对这次友好的会面感到惊奇。大部分时间里，两个人都在讨论南非历史，尽管观点迥异。最后，曼德拉将话题引到更加重要的事务上。他阐明，除非政治犯被无条件释放，否则真正的协商无从谈起。

不出所料，博塔告知曼德拉，政府无法满足他的要求。事实上，这次会面最终没有实质性的结果。然而，曼德拉对会面感到满意。他意识到，外部的压力以及社会的不稳定，终于对统治者产生危害。他梦想的新南非即将变成现实。

然而，事态变得不太明朗，因为博塔一个月后就辞职下台了。辞职使得曼德拉与政

[1] do their bidding
听命于

[2] renounce 放弃

[3] taking their toll
造成损失（或危害、伤亡等）

later. The resignation threw the ongoing negotiations between Mandela and the government into a quandary[1]. A cabinet member, F. W. de Klerk, was sworn in as acting president. He was an unknown and nothing in his past suggested that he'd be any more sympathetic to the black cause than others in the government had been. Still, negotiations continued.

Mandela held firm to his demands. As de Klerk was sworn in as president, Mandela again requested that all political prisoners be released. In exchange for a democratic and racially free South Africa, Mandela promised disciplined behavior from the black leadership.

Mandela watched the new president and sized him up[2]. He was made hopeful by what he saw. When faced with a demonstration, de Klerk did not ban the leaders as his predecessors had. He simply instructed the leaders to make the demonstration peaceful. That, in itself, was a change.

Finally, in October of 1989, de Klerk did something Mandela had waited nearly three decades to see. He released a number of political prisoners. Among them was Mandela's longtime friend and mentor, Walter Sisulu. That action laid the foundation for a meeting between the president and Mandela on December 12.

Unlike the meeting with Botha, this one actually bore fruit. The two men did not always see eye-to-eye, but de Klerk was someone with whom Mandela could do business. Mandela later described de Klerk as a

thoughtful man who was willing to listen and think matters through. He made none of the knee-jerk[3] reactions Mandela had come to expect from authorities.

One point that stood as an obstacle, however, was the president's idea of "group rights." This concept would essentially preserve power for white South Africans, regardless of election outcomes. Mandela would not

府间正在进行的谈判陷入了进退两难的境地。内阁成员德克勒克宣誓就任代理总统。他并不出名，从他以前的经历中也看不出他在黑人问题上比其他政府官员抱有更多的同情心。尽管如此，谈判仍在继续。

曼德拉对自己的要求立场坚定。当德克勒克宣誓就任总统时，曼德拉又一次要求释放所有政治犯。为换取南非的民主与种族自由，曼德拉承诺黑人领袖们将会克制自己的行为。

曼德拉观察新总统，并对他作了估计。他所看到的使他产生了希望。在应对示威活动时，德克勒克没有像他的那些前任一样对运动领袖下禁令。他只是命令运动领袖要和平举行示威活动。这样的应对方式本身就是一种改变。

最终，在1989年10月，德克勒克做出了曼德拉已等待了将近30年的举动。他释放了大量政治犯，其中包括曼德拉多年的良师益友瓦尔特·西苏卢。这一举动奠定了总统与曼德拉在12月12日会面的基础。

和那次与博塔的会面不同，这次会面终于有了成果。两个人并不总是意见相投，但是德克勒克的确是曼德拉可与之一起解决问题的人。曼德拉后来形容德克勒克是一个考虑周到的人，乐意倾听并会对问题进行深思熟虑。他没有做出那种曼德拉料想当权者会做出的容易预测的反应。

不过，有一点成了双方的一道障碍，就是总统提出的"集团权利"的想法。这一概念将从根本上保持南非白人的特权，无论选举结果如何。曼德拉不会接受这一想法。对

[1] quandary 困惑；进退两难的境地

[2] sized him up 评价，估计

[3] knee-jerk （反应等）自动的，容易预测的，机械的

纳尔逊·曼德拉

accept this idea. It looked to him like the government was not really willing to end apartheid—only to modify it.

After some thought, de Klerk acknowledged that the government's position could be adjusted. On February 2, 1990, he made it clear that he was sincere. Before Parliament, he announced sweeping changes that would dismantle[1] apartheid. He announced that the government would lift the bans on the ANC, the Communist Party, and the Pan African Congress, as well as thirty-one other organizations. The government would also free political prisoners, suspend capital punishment, and lift other restrictions.

A week later, de Klerk was back with Mandela, explaining that he would be released from prison the next day. There would be no restrictions placed on Mandela; he would be free to continue his political activity.

On February 11, 1990, after twenty-seven years in prison, Nelson Mandela was free. In the great square in front of City Hall in Cape Town, a throng of people greeted him. There was thunderous applause as Mandela stepped to the microphone, his wife Winnie at his side, and raised his fist in victory. "*Amandla*," he shouted. "*Ngawethu*," the crowd called back.

The air was charged with excitement and power. The hero of the African liberation struggle stood before the crowd. Generations had grown up without seeing his face, only hearing his name in whispers. Now here he was, older, but fit, trim[2], and full of life.

"Friends, comrades, and fellow South Africans," he started in a clear voice. These were the first public words he had uttered since his trial decades earlier. "I greet you

NELSON MANDELA

他来说，这种想法看起来像是政府并不想真的废除种族隔离制度——只是对其进行修改。

经过考虑，德克勒克承认，政府的立场可以进行调整。1990年2月2日，他明确表示出自己的诚意。在议会上，他宣布了彻底取消种族隔离制度的改革措施。他宣布，政府将解除对非国大、共产党、泛非大会以及其他31个组织的禁令。政府还将释放政治犯，缓期执行死刑，同时取消其他限制。

一周后，德克勒克又回来见曼德拉，告诉他，他将在第二天获释。将不会再有针对曼德拉的禁令；他将不受限制地继续自己的政治活动。

1990年2月11日，在狱中度过了27年后，纳尔逊·曼德拉自由了。在开普敦市政厅前的大广场上，群众在迎接他。当曼德拉和妻子温妮走向麦克风并以胜利的姿态举起拳头时，人群爆发出雷鸣般的掌声。"力量，"他大喊。"力量属于我们，"人群回应道。

空气中充满着激情与力量。非洲自由斗争的英雄立于人群之前。几代人在成长的过程中都没有见过他的模样，只是在传闻中听过他的名字。现在他就在这里，变老了，但健康，整洁，充满生命力。

"朋友们，同志们，南非的同胞们，"他用清晰的嗓音开始发言。这是自从几十年前的审判以来他在公众面前说出的第一句话。"我以所有人的和平、民主与自由的名义向你

[1] dismantle （逐渐）结束（体制等）

[2] trim 整洁的

纳尔逊·曼德拉

all in the name of peace, democracy and freedom for all. I stand before you not as a prophet[1] but as a humble servant of you, the people."

He saluted the people and the various groups that had worked to end the injustice of apartheid. He praised all who had fought and died in the struggle. He praised the heroism of students who had resisted when their parents no longer had the will to fight. He praised his comrades in the ANC and other organizations that had worked for justice. He also praised the international community for its sanctions against South Africa:

Today the majority of South Africans, black and white, recognize that apartheid has no future. It has to be ended by our own decisive mass action in order to build peace and security....The destruction caused by apartheid on our subcontinent is incalculable. The fabric of family life of millions of my people has been shattered. Millions are homeless and unemployed. Our economy lies in ruins and our people are embroiled[2] in political strife[3].... The factors which necessitated the armed struggle still exist today. We have no option but to continue. We express the hope that a climate conducive[4] to a negotiated settlement will be created soon so that there may no longer be the need for the armed struggle.

Mandela went on to Soweto and greeted another massive gathering in the soccer stadium there. Many in the audience were youths who had witnessed the protests in and around their township. They, too, lifted the spirits of their hero with the sound of their cheers.

Shortly after the fanfare surrounding his release had died down, Mandela reported to the ANC leadership about the state of negotiations with the government. Members of the Executive Committee were pleased to see him free, but there were questions in their eyes. They wondered if Mandela was the

NELSON MANDELA

[1] prophet （新思想、主义等的）宣扬者; 提倡者

[2] embroiled 卷入
[3] strife 斗争

[4] conducive 有助于……的

纳尔逊·曼德拉

们致敬。我站在你们面前，不是作为宣扬者，而是作为你们人民的卑微的仆人。"

他向为终结不平等的种族隔离制度而奋斗的组织和人民致敬。他赞扬了所有在斗争中奋斗、牺牲的人。他赞扬了学生的英雄品质，当他们的父母都失去了战斗的欲望时，他们却坚持抗争。他赞扬了非国大的同志，以及其他为公正做出贡献的组织。他同时也因为对南非实行的制裁而赞扬了国际社会：

今天，大多数的南非人，无论是黑人还是白人，都意识到种族隔离制度没有未来。它必须由我们自己决定性的群众行动去终结，从而建立和平与安全……种族隔离制度在我们这片次大陆上造成的破坏难以估量。我无数人民的家庭生活的结构遭到破坏。无数人无家可归并失业。我们的经济被毁灭，我们的人民卷入政治斗争……必须进行武装斗争的种种因素在今天依然存在。我们别无选择，只有继续进行斗争。我们希望，不久将能创造出一种有利于通过谈判解决问题的气氛，以便不再有必要开展武装斗争。

曼德拉随后来到索韦托，在一个足球场里问候另一批集会的人群。听众中有不少年轻人，他们亲眼见证了发生在他们社区内外的抗议活动。他们的欢呼声也使他们的英雄情绪高涨。

当他获释后的欢迎仪式逐渐结束后不久，曼德拉就向非国大领导层汇报了与政府谈判的情况。看到他获得自由，执行委员会的委员们很高兴，但是他们存有疑虑。他们

same man who had gone to prison. Had he been broken? Had he sold out[1]? Mandela understood the questions. He had been isolated for a long time. But he put the leaders' fears to rest, and by the end of the meeting he was elected deputy president of the ANC.

Having regained the confidence of his colleagues, Mandela went abroad and met with leaders throughout Africa, Europe, and America. He was amazed at the enthusiastic responses wherever he went. Even the most conservative leaders, those who had criticized the ANC in the past, welcomed him. They were impressed with him not only for his conviction and great intellect but also for his lack of bitterness toward those who had imprisoned him. Mandela did not focus on revenge but only upon what was best for the future of his country.

Unfortunately, while his public life was a series of successes, his family life was difficult. Winnie was on a different political track. As Nelson worked to bring all South Africans together, Winnie was more confrontational toward the government. Her brand of radicalism seemed counterproductive[2] to many within the ANC. The couple had also drifted apart in personal ways. In April 1992, Mandela announced that he and Winnie had separated. He was careful to explain that he still loved and respected her.

In a painful revelation, Mandela realized that he was married to the

struggle and was father to a nation. He regretted the pain his family had experienced. But apartheid had destroyed the lives and families of millions of others, as well. Though his sacrifices were great, they had to be made if a new nation were to come into being.

Throughout his personal difficulties, Mandela stayed on course politically. He

NELSON MANDELA

想知道，曼德拉还是不是入狱前的那个人了。他被打垮了吗？他背叛了吗？曼德拉很理解这些疑虑。他已经被与世隔绝了很长一段时间。不过他打消了领导们的担忧，会议结束前，他被选为非国大副主席。

重新赢得了同事们的信任后，曼德拉出国遍访了非洲、欧洲以及美洲的领导人。他所到之处无不反响热烈，他对此感到惊讶。即便是最保守的领导人，就是那些从前批评过非国大的人，都对他表示了欢迎。他们不仅对他的信念与智慧印象深刻，更让他们难忘的是，他对因禁自己的人没有心存愤恨。曼德拉不专注于复仇，他只想着什么对于自己国家的将来是最好的。

很不幸，正当他的公共活动取得了一系列成功的时候，他的家庭生活却出现了困难。温妮走上了不同的政治道路。在纳尔逊致力于团结整个南非的时候，温妮却对政府采取更为敌对的态度。对非国大里很多人来说，她那特有的激进主义似乎产生了相反的效果。私下里，这对夫妻也已经彼此疏远了。1992年4月，曼德拉宣布他与温妮已经分居。他小心地解释说他仍然爱着她，尊重她。

在令人痛苦的真相面前，曼德拉意识到自己已与斗争结婚，成了国家的父亲。他对于他的家庭所遭受的痛苦深感遗憾。但是，种族隔离制度同样已经摧毁了其他无数人的生命与家庭。虽然他的自我牺牲十分巨大，但是如果要形成一个新的国家，这样的牺牲是无法避免的。

不顾种种个人困难，曼德拉坚持已有的政

[1] sold out （特别是为了钱）背叛

[2] counterproductive 导致相反结果的，产生相反效果的

纳尔逊·曼德拉

negotiated with the government to create a new political structure. Negotiations were not always easy. Radical forces on both sides tried to disrupt the process. However, on June 3, 1993, Mandela presented a formula for a new political system that gave rights to all South Africans. The first national, racially unrestricted, one-person-one-vote election would be held the following year.

It was a historic turning point. Mandela and President de Klerk were both rewarded for their efforts later in 1993, when they jointly accepted the Nobel Prize for Peace. As they stood together in Oslo, Norway, Mandela applauded de Klerk's efforts as a partner in moving the nation beyond the dark past of racial hatred.

Ironically, the two men who raised hands together in Oslo then became political rivals back home. The dismantling of apartheid prompted the first election in which all South Africans could participate. The black majority finally had a say in the running of their country, and the man they wanted for president was Nelson Mandela. On May 2, 1994, Mandela won the election and became the first black president of South Africa. He made it his duty to heal the wounds of the past.

"This is one of the most important moments in the life of our country," he said during his victory speech. "I stand here before you filled with deep pride and joy—pride in the ordinary, humble people of this country.

You have shown such a calm, patient determination to reclaim this country as your own, and now the joy that we can loudly proclaim from the rooftops—Free at last! Free at last! I stand before you, humbled by your courage, with a heart full of love for all of you....This is a time to heal the old wounds and build a new South Africa."

A week later, as Nelson Mandela was

治方针。他与政府展开谈判，要求建立全新的政治体制。谈判并不总是顺利。谈判双方的激进势力都在试图破坏谈判进程。尽管如此，在1993年6月3日，曼德拉还是提出了一套构筑全新政治体制的方案，在新体制中，所有的南非人都享有权利。第一届全国性的、对种族不加以限制的、一人一票制的选举将在次年举行。

这是历史性的转折点。曼德拉与德克勒克总统因他们的努力，于1993年共同获得诺贝尔和平奖。在挪威奥斯陆，当他们站在一起时，曼德拉把德克勒克的努力称赞为使国家超越种族仇恨这阴暗过去的伙伴。

具有讽刺意味的是，这两位携手奥斯陆的人，回到祖国后就成了政治对手。种族隔离制度的废除促成了第一次所有南非人都可以参加的选举。占多数的黑人最终对国家的治理有了发言权，他们希望当选总统的人就是纳尔逊·曼德拉。1994年5月2日，曼德拉赢得大选，成为南非第一位黑人总统。他将治愈历史的创伤作为自己的责任。

"这是我们国家历史上最重要的时刻之一，"他在胜选演讲中说。"我站在此地，面对大家，充满着深深的自豪与喜悦——为这个国家平凡而谦卑的人民感到自豪。你们表现出如此的镇静与耐心，做出决定，收回这个国家并成为主人，同时收回一种喜悦，这是种我们现在可以从屋顶大声宣布的喜悦——终于自由了！终于自由了！我站在你们面前，被你们的勇气折服，心中充满着对你们所有人的爱意……现在是时候治愈旧的创伤了，是时候建设新的南非了。"

一周后，当纳尔逊·曼德拉宣誓就职时，看到

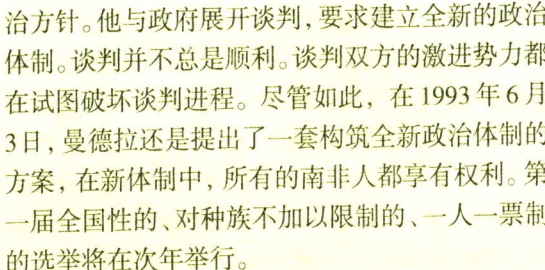

纳尔逊·曼德拉

being sworn into office, he looked out upon a sea of faces. There were leaders from around the world, journalists, and comrades in the struggle. All looked on as this man of dignity and strength took the oath of office and addressed the crowd:

Out of the experience of an extraordinary human disaster that lasted too long, must be born a society of which all humanity will be proud.... We have, at last, achieved our political emancipation[1]. We pledge ourselves to liberate all our people from the continuing bondage of poverty, deprivation, suffering, gender, and other discrimination. Never, never, and never again shall it be that this beautiful land will again experience the oppression of one by another....The sun shall never set on so glorious a human achievement.

Let freedom reign. God bless Africa!

NELSON MANDELA

外面人山人海。其中包括世界各国的首脑、记者，以及斗争中的同志。所有人都在一旁观看着，这位有着尊严与力量的男人宣誓就职，进而对观众发表演说：

在经历了非同寻常的、过于漫长的人类的灾难后，一个让全人类感到骄傲的社会必将诞生……我们终于获得了我们自己的政治解放。我们立誓将我们所有的人民从继续存在着的束缚中解放出来，它们包括贫穷、剥夺、苦难、性别以及其他种种歧视。永远，永远，永远也不会，在这片美丽的土地上，再出现人压迫人的现象……太阳将永不离开人类所取得的这一光辉成就。

让自由成为主宰。上帝保佑非洲！

[1] emancipation
解放

纳尔逊·曼德拉